LOOK

ALSO BY CHRISTIAN MADSBJERG

The Moment of Clarity:
Using the Human Sciences to Solve Your Toughest
Business Problems (with Mikkel B. Rasmussen)

Sensemaking:
The Power of the Humanities
in the Age of the Algorithm

LOOK

How to Pay Attention
in a Distracted World

· ·

CHRISTIAN MADSBJERG

RIVERHEAD BOOKS   NEW YORK   2023

RIVERHEAD BOOKS
An imprint of Penguin Random House LLC
penguinrandomhouse.com

Grateful acknowledgment is made for permission to reprint the following:

Excerpts from *The Peregrine* by J. A. Baker. Copyright © 1967 by J. A. Baker.
Reprinted by permission of HarperCollins Publishers, Ltd.

Excerpts from *Things: A Story of the Sixties* by George Perec, translated by
Davis Bellos. Copyright © 1965 by René Julliard. Translation copyright © 1990 by
Wm. Collins Sons & Co., Ltd. Reprinted with the permission of The Permissions Company,
LLC on behalf of David R Godine, Publisher, Inc., www.godine.com.

LIBRARY OF CONGRESS CATALOGING-IN-PUBLICATION DATA

Names: Madsbjerg, Christian, author.
Title: Look : how to pay attention in a distracted world / Christian Madsbjerg.
Description: New York : Riverhead Books, 2023. | Includes index.
Identifiers: LCCN 2023001867 (print) | LCCN 2023001868 (ebook) | ISBN 9780593542217 (hardcover) |
ISBN 9780593714676 (trade paperback) | ISBN 9780593542231 (ebook)
Subjects: LCSH: Attention. | Distraction (Psychology) | Observation (Psychology)
Classification: LCC BF321 .M27 2023 (print) | LCC BF321 (ebook) |
DDC 153.7/33—dc23/eng/20230411
LC record available at https://lccn.loc.gov/2023001867
LC ebook record available at https://lccn.loc.gov/2023001868

Printed in the United States of America
1st Printing

Book design by Daniel Lagin

To Saadia

CONTENTS

PART TWO
GETTING STARTED

ESSAYS AND THOUGHTS
EXERCISES TO INSPIRE YOUR PRACTICE

What determines our judgment, our concepts and reactions, is not what one man is doing now, an individual action, but the whole hurly-burly of human actions, the background against which we see any action.

—Ludwig Wittgenstein

INTRODUCTION

The Most Difficult Thing to
See Is What Is Really There

1.

A journalist arrives in a small Italian city to cover a student protest. She dutifully takes notes describing the angry rioting of the young people: "How dare the city make budget cuts to university spending given the increasingly tight labor market?" She gives her entire day to conducting dozens of interviews with the young people camping out along the picket lines in the town square. She can see a story taking shape about an increasingly desperate youth culture getting squeezed out by wage decreases and fewer university spots. In the distractions of the protest, however, she misses seeing who is standing at the outskirts of the square. There, in the darkness, hundreds of older men and women stand silent. This older generation once worked on the land and cultivated skills that were valued in factories and farms. Now they are on the sidelines, forgotten and irrelevant, their opinions and concerns deemed worthless by the youth. The journalist was so caught up in capturing those who were shouting that she missed those who stood in silence. She filed a small story about a single student protest while missing the much larger story about the rise of Far Right fascism across Italy.

2.

An executive at a multinational electronics company guided his department to market leadership in the television industry. For more than a decade, he focused all his energy on making televisions with bigger screens and clearer image resolution. He worked with hundreds of engineers on his team to innovate in areas like light efficiency, wider color spectrums, and breakthroughs in HD. His group filed thousands of patents as they became known as the industry gold standard in screen technology. While he was paying attention to higher fidelity in the screen experience, however, he missed seeing how the world of watching was changing around him. Instead of seeking out televisions with greater resolution, people were spending more time watching their favorite shows on laptops and mobile phones. He had bet the future of the company on improving screens while completely missing how the human experience of those screens was changing. People didn't want the screen with the best image quality; they wanted the screen that could fit inside their pockets while giving them constant connectivity. How did he miss seeing it?

3.

A professor of social work runs an acclaimed research program at a city university to train caseworkers. Lately, however, when he goes out to observe his mentees working in the city's bureaucracies, he finds that their time with clients is stiff and rushed. His mentees immediately ask questions to complete their paperwork and spend little to no time getting to know their clients. At first, the professor thought the social workers needed more guidance, so he encouraged them to take a few minutes at the beginning of each of their interactions to connect with their clients. Make eye contact, he suggested. Ask your clients about their day, try to engage in some warm pleasantries. He gave them robust data that showed that these small gestures created more trust between clients and caseworkers. The social workers were not so easily convinced. Their managers were counting on them to deliver a certain number of cases every week with all the questions and issues properly addressed. Their meetings with clients needed to focus on extracting data for the paperwork, not engaging in useless chitchat. The professor tried to convince them otherwise, but the caseworkers remained skeptical. They were worried they would never get their real work done. It occurred to the professor that he had failed to convince the people working in social work of *the value of being social.*

I share these stories to help you understand the importance of learning how to pay attention to our human world. In each one, highly skilled professionals miss seeing the most important aspects of the context they are working in and on. As a result, they flounder and fail without understanding why. Their efforts never actually create any meaningful change. They simply don't know how to discern what matters.

I want you to know that understanding the social context of our world is the most important path you can take to arrive at meaningful insights. When you learn how to observe both the background and the foreground, you will train yourself to see what really matters to yourself and to other people.

But what is the background? How do we define it? Philosophers and thinkers have been trying to answer this question for more than one hundred years, but the best answer is that the background is where we absorb all our behaviors, practices, ideas, and habits. Ludwig Wittgenstein, one of the more modern philosophers exploring this idea, argued that "what determines our judgment, our concepts and reactions, is not what one man is doing now, an individual action, but the whole hurly-burly of human actions, the background against which we see any action."

The background—or *the hurly-burly*—is nothing less than an understanding of how people make sense of the world they're living in. It is the patterns and structures of behavior that guide our everyday actions and decisions, which are so familiar to the people absorbed in them that they never even pay attention to them. If a fish were a philosopher, it would describe this background—the hurly-burly—as "water."

What is incredible is that each of us can bring an awareness to this so-called hurly-burly and learn to observe it analytically. This is a meta-skill that is called "hyper-reflection," and in this book I will walk you through how it works. Developing this type of rigorous observational practice will transform your experience of everyday life. Whether you are designing megacities or metaverses, dealing with your constituents or trying to make a deal with your colleagues, navigating the climate crisis or simply trying to navigate your children's schooling, you will be more successful if you take the time to learn how to see and understand this background—the whole hurly-burly of human action. This kind of direct observation does not rely on models, theories, or any other abstract layer over our experience, and that is why it is the most accurate way to understand how and why we humans do what we do.

Most people don't even take the time to acknowledge that the background is there. This is unfortunate, for when you learn to see that it exists, it gives you a secret power of understanding. The richest reality is revealed, and you start paying attention to what is most relevant. In this book, I will show you how to cultivate this power and use it to solve challenges both big and small.

It all begins with looking. Don't think, look.

LOOK

HOW TO LOOK

I spend most of my professional life looking and listening. More than two decades ago, I co-founded a company called ReD Associates because I wanted to connect our group of social science researchers—trained in disciplines like anthropology, sociology, and philosophy—with organizations that needed highly skilled observers. I could see that leaders of some of the world's most powerful companies were often woefully disconnected from the people they served. Without really understanding how to truly observe, they had become unmoored, relying too much on the abstractions of quantitative analysis and the perils of groupthink. My job was to help them reconnect with the power of human interpretation: relearning ways to look and listen to others with focus and care.

When done well, these skills can snap an entire strategy into focus, create new possibilities in artistic, scientific, and business contexts, and inspire everyone in the room to see the possibilities of a different reality. Whether an observation makes you burst out laughing, start to sob, or commit to changing your life, insightful observations inevitably lead you to say, "That is so true." This truth is not a universal law from the world of natural science—humans are nonlinear and strange compared with atoms or asteroids—but it will tell you something profound about how an event is being experienced. When we identify what is true, it has the power to shed light onto how something or someone works.

After all my years working with observational skills, one question kept returning to me: Can this kind of direct observation be taught? I knew from hiring more than a thousand people that good observers share certain characteristics. The best observers are thoughtful and rarely rush to conclusions. They are also highly organized and are driven not by their opinions but by what they see. There is a tenderness but also something regimented to great observers. Given all this, could I help people with an inclination toward astute observations get better at it with practice? If I could, what would that practice look like? Can hyper-reflection be taught?

In 2015, my friend Simon Critchley, a world-famous philosopher, a professor at the New School, and editor of the *New York Times*'s long-running opinion series the Stone, together with Tim Marshall, the provost at the New School, asked me to co-teach a course with him that explored these questions. We imaginatively called it Human Observation.

Designing the reading and exercises for the course gave me the perfect opportunity to experiment with answers to my questions. If an observational practice can be taught, what skills are at its heart? What exercises should we use? And because observation is only one thread in a greater exploration of how we understand the world and draw meaning from it, what are the other essential threads for appreciating observation at its most profound level?

When Simon and I created the course, we imagined speaking to a small group of philosophy students sitting around a seminar table. Instead, from its very first semester, Human Observation has been oversubscribed with hundreds of students eager to enroll from across the graduate and undergraduate programs, with a long wait list to get in. The students came from all over the school: liberal arts, business, performing arts, design, and all categories of the social sciences and humanities.

While we were delighted by the students' enthusiasm, Simon and I were also surprised. This was not the response we usually received at the announcement of a new course. Once I started teaching the class, however, I realized why these students were so eager to learn how to pay attention, listen, and observe. They were experiencing the same disoriented feelings that I had identified in the executives I met over years of consulting. There was a hunger in them to learn, once again, how to see the world. The more time I spent with these students, the more I realized how pervasive these experiences were in the culture at large. Almost all of us feel isolated from the practice of direct observation. Why?

In this book, I offer you my answer to this question. I find that most of us are looking in the wrong places and at the wrong things. Our attention is on what is happening in the foreground—whether the foreground is the person with the loudest voice in the room, the commodity with the biggest drop, or the technology trend with the largest number of users. This kind of foregrounded attention leaves us feeling drained and confused. What we are looking at does not bring us any closer to an understanding of reality.

When we bring our attention to seeing and analyzing the background, however, profound insights start to snap into place. This background, or the hurly-burly, tells us nothing about who said what and where they said it—the foreground of reality—but it reveals everything about how and why people do the things they do. It is the invisible scaffolding that surrounds all of us and guides our actions and behaviors. Most people don't even understand that this background exists, and very few people take the time to learn how to observe it analytically. This is precisely why many of us feel so distracted and unproductive when we look at our world. We are trying to see the vista out the window, but most of us are stuck staring at a dirty windowpane. No wonder we all feel so uninspired.

Fortunately for all of us, a coterie of brilliant philosophers, anthropologists, and artists have paved the way for our inquiry. They have given us a set of techniques and tools for observing and analyzing the background. I have translated their work, much of it dense and difficult to read, into an accessible practice called hyper-reflection. In it, you learn to see not the next bright, shiny bauble that catches your eye but the hidden social structures that explain what that bauble means, why it is here, and where it is headed.

In that first class several years ago and in the subsequent sessions of it that I have taught, my students found transformative results with this practice. Our work together confirmed that people of all ages and from all walks of life can learn and improve upon this kind of observation. By engaging with the ideas that most inspire me as well as the artists, writers, and thinkers who've mastered these observational skills, we can all get better at seeing the world around us. Learning to see our reality as it actually exists is a skill that will change your life. This book is an invitation to you to find out how.

WHAT IS OBSERVATION?

Observation as a skill sounds straightforward, but most of us are getting it wrong. We are putting all our energies into observing events in the foreground rather than taking the time to analytically understand how to see the background as well. In the first part of this book, "The Foundation of the Practice," I will walk you through the philosophical foundation for cultivating a meta-skill like hyper-reflection. In some sections, I'll use stories to help you understand my arguments. In other places, I'll offer you my own interpretation of the philosophy that excites me the most. In every example, however, I share only what I think will serve you in developing your practice of hyper-reflection. My goal is not to write about philosophy for philosophers. I want to show you how to *use* philosophy in your everyday life.

In addition to philosophical inspiration, I will also introduce you to observational masterpieces that changed the way I look at the world. These are the books that make up the core of the class. They have helped me, my many associates over the years, and the hundreds of students I have taught. I am confident they will open up new ways of thinking for you too.

The second part of this book, "Getting Started," will provide you with brief thought pieces accompanied by prompts, provocations, and inspirations designed to guide you in your practice. Some of these examples may surprise you, but all of them helped me understand how the craft of great observation works.

The three building blocks that we will return to in every chapter all draw from a philosophical approach called phenomenology, which is the study of how we experience the world.

HOW DO WE STUDY EXPERIENCES?

Phenomenology is "the science of phenomena" and is perhaps the most important philosophical tradition of the twentieth century. At its core, it claims that describing the human experience of "things" directly without any filters is possible, and that this description gives us a much better understanding of what it means to be human. We are not looking to understand what any individual feels in a particular moment but rather the whole structure of the way we experience the world. Based on *what* do we do what we do? The founders of this tradition argue that we humans rarely think abstractly and analytically about life happening around us. We understand very keenly how our world works, but we rarely think about it. In essence, phenomenology is the study of how the human world works and everything that gives our lives meaning.

Phenomenology can unlock the experience of living in a city or the sensation of being a mother. It is whether we see an American flag and regard it with nostalgia and trust or with disdain and anger. As a tool, it can describe the experience of a thing like a truck. Any truck has a weight, color, and shape. Trucks have a physical limit to how fast they can drive and how much they can tow that we can measure. We can think about these data points, but they say very little about what role a truck plays in our lives and communities. Such facts are particularly poor at describing the actual act of driving the truck. As drivers, we engage directly in driving without truly thinking analytically about it. This total immersion in the world of what we "do" rather than "think" is a core tenet of phenomenology. Experience rarely has anything to do with thinking and almost everything to do with being engaged actively in the world.

This might sound unscientific, but it is a highly organized way to explore what things mean to us and how we use different types of equipment in our lives. If you visit a jeweler and show him a diamond ring, for example, he will assess the number of carats in it. That number will give you information about the scientific constitution of the stone, but only phenomenology will shed light on your experience of those carats. What role does this glorified rock play in our lives? Does it make us feel safe? Overwhelmed? Ashamed? Loved? What does it mean to wear it on your hand? How do you feel when you walk around with it? And what are those experiences based on?

What we are interested in is what is most familiar to us, so familiar that it structures our behavior without ever being something we think about. It feels so normal and true, but when we look at it directly, it often is rather odd. When I use the word *background*, I am referring to the way all of us have a familiarity with the worlds we know well. We stop seeing the background because it is so familiar to us. As observers, we want to analyze what is familiar to people and find out how and why it works.

Consider another example of phenomenology. An hour is always sixty minutes, and 11:00 a.m. is the same time (roughly) every day, but a minute can be experienced as an hour, and an 11:00 a.m. meeting can feel like it is starting at the beginning of the day. How long is a minute in experience time rather than clock time? The abstract measurement of time increments reveals nothing about the way we experience that time. What is it like to live through this one specific minute in this one very specific context? What is our experience of that 11:00 a.m. meeting?

If all of this strikes you as decidedly *un*scientific—after all, how can you make a science out of the way things are experienced by one person somewhere in the world?—consider it in a different way. Phenomenology will not reveal the essence of something—a car, for example, or a piece of jewelry, or a restaurant—but rather the essence of our shared *relationship* to that thing. Not everything is important to us all the time. We stand in relationship to the things in our lives, and phenomenology can show us which things matter most and when.

Take the concept of money. Instead of examining it in the physical world—as cellulose with ink printed on it—try to examine it in the human world. Money is a shared language for value. Most of us prefer having more of it rather than having less. Many of us are afraid of it. Some find it arousing, while certain cultures refuse to speak of it out loud or even acknowledge its existence. When banks design accounts for their customers, they typically give people with more money greater access to it. In a banker's world, it is vital for top clients to have full transparency with their accounts. But if you look more closely at how wealthy people *experience* their money—how they have it or spend it—a banker's perspective may not be the most appropriate mindset for designing an account. After all, most people with money don't want to see it every day. They want to be assured that it is safe, but they don't have any interest in counting it the way bankers do. In this way, bankers miss an opportunity to have more meaningful relationships with the people they serve because they impose their values on their clients.

The slogan of phenomenology is "To the thing itself." The idea is to study the thing itself—be it a work of literature, death, family, a car, a vaccine, or the hospital—without preconceived notions, trendy easy

8

answers, or dogma imposed on it. This is how we begin to arrive at the types of observations that lead to insights.

Think of a recent moment when you decided to buy a new house, quit your job, or get married. You might have ideas or stories you tell yourself about how you made the decision, but try scraping away these conceits and examine your genuine experience. How did you—really—go from the experience of "not knowing" to "making a decision"? For example, how did you honestly make choices about this year's budget? When did you truly decide to start a relationship or have a family? How did you arrive at the decision to move or to change jobs?

I would guess that most of these decisions were made not in an entirely rational way, but from below the level of conscious thought. Now you can bring some rigor to observing and describing that experience. What is it based on? This is where the study of experiences really begins: with direct first-person experience. It's not a license to navel gaze, however, because the subjective experience is only the beginning. You use it to think about how to uncover patterns occurring in the picture as a whole. Phenomenology is not interested in what is extraordinary, but in what is ordinary, familiar, and common for all (or most) of us. In this way, it isn't about polling large numbers of people or finding the biggest sample size. Each common and ordinary human experience can be collected and examined to fully understand the patterns of behavior we all share.

In this way, the study of experience is neither just about you and your subjective reality nor just about what happens in the scientific world of "objective reality." The art and science of great observations flourish in the space between these two. We might call that space the "intersubjective," what happens between us and the world of others.

This is our shared world and the place of relationships, and great observations reveal something truthful about how we relate to it. The best observers are not asking: What is happening? They are asking: How are we experiencing it?

If you tend to understand your world primarily through statistics, trend pieces, spreadsheets, or any other kind of abstract framework, then the study of experiences gives you a chance to refresh your perspective. I love statistics, and I find breakthroughs in science and technology thrilling, but we need a better starting point than either of these frameworks. Instead of beginning an inquiry by looking at numbers or a preformed hypothesis, start with direct observation. Strip away the received wisdom and assumptions and take stock of what your observations reveal about the rich reality of the world we all share.

IT'S NOT *WHAT* PEOPLE THINK; IT'S HOW

Our job as observers is not to pay attention to what other people think. Why? When you really reflect on most of the conversations occurring all around you, you already know that people say things they don't mean all the time. The best observers take note of what people say, but they don't put great stake in it. The observer's role is to move beyond what's said or done to truly understand why people behave the way they do. We want to get an understanding of the whole picture: How do people think? What do they believe to be true? Where is the key that opens the portal to a wider understanding? What makes us do the things we do?

Take the difference in child-rearing in the city where I spent most of my young adult life, Copenhagen, and the culture of where I live now in New York City. If you want to gain a better understanding of how child-rearing works, you would be missing something essential by seeing only the *what*: the percentage of children in day care, for example, or the number of children, on average, in each Danish family. You also can't ask Danish people in Copenhagen to consciously explain their experience of raising children. They will tell you all sorts of curious details about their personal parenting philosophies—how fresh eggs will make children smarter or how a brisk walk will make a cold disappear—many of which bear little resemblance to their behavior. Paying attention to these scraps of information won't give you an accurate picture of the whole experience of raising children in Copenhagen. These details are akin to settling for mere bread crumbs, while the best observers know they are seeking the whole loaf and the recipe for how it is made. The careful observer listens for the *how* in Danish thinking. This "how"—the whole picture—is the idea of *exposure*.

Danish children are regularly exposed to the elements of nature— most days outside, winter and summer. They are exposed to fighting— sometimes intense—between packs of kids, with no intervention from adults. There are fewer anti-bullying campaigns, fewer concerns about peanut allergies, fewer consensus-building huddles, and no trophies for participating. Danish children are deliberately exposed to all types of opinions and language because that is how one lives in a country with a safety net of support. In Copenhagen, parents move through the world trying to expose their children to as much as possible. This is "how" they think.

On the other hand, where my own children are growing up in New York City, the "how" of thinking is *protection*. Children are protected from germs, from bullies, from harmful opinions and language deemed "violent" against them or others. To raise children in this world is to believe that childhood is inherently innocent and best managed with regular protective interventions from adults. To better understand the difference between the two approaches, consider the analogy of food: most European cultures tend to think about food as a living entity with aspects of rot that are desirable in the form of cheese and other fermentation. Mainstream American food culture, on the other hand, tries to protect food with pasteurization, favoring purity, safety, and longevity over this natural decay. In this way, children in the city of my youth are left alone with less intervention, while in New York they are ushered away from conflict through the protection of adults.

This kind of whole-picture understanding will not appear to an observer immediately. Unlike a Polaroid that materializes a clear image in seconds, the whole-picture insight of great observations takes patience and analytical rigor. Along the way, even the best observers are vulnerable to the distracting red herrings of "what" people say. This is where phenomenology grounds us. We are always returning to the phenomenon—in this case, "child-rearing"—and looking for the behavior and unarticulated beliefs that structure it. When you begin an observation, you will hear "what" immediately. Don't be misled. It is imperative to wait for a key to unlock the portal: "How does this world work?" This is how another reality reveals itself to us.

OBSERVATION IS NOT OPINION

My students have been taught to believe that opinions come first and that critical analysis follows. In our work together, I encourage them to put the impulse to opine on pause. There is certainly a time and place for opinions, but it is never in the earliest stages of an observational process. We need to notice, see, watch, observe, not conclude.

Begin and end with description, not opinion. The heart of good observation is not to try to uplift or persuade. It is certainly not to cast aspersions. In all the best observations, morality is of no interest, and descriptions are detached from good or bad feelings about people involved. What you think—or what I think—is not the point. Isn't that a relief?

So much of our daily life requires us to make up our minds. What will we cook for dinner? How much time will we allow our children on the computer? What do we think about the new housing development that's being built down the street? When our goal is observation and not opinion, it is akin to saying that we are "not making up our minds." This can feel incredibly uncomfortable. Many of my students feel anxious, and some of them even feel nauseated when they directly observe the world without any political framework. We all crave some sense of certainty about what we see, but it is this certainty that impairs our ability to discern the truth. When you start with the intention to *not* make up your mind, or when you work to directly undermine your own assumptions to prove yourself wrong, you will see your own perception at work.

Once you grow more comfortable with this stillness, the act of suspending judgment is liberating. Instead of opining or jumping into a theory, the best observers wait, watch, and describe—in the process they come to see what mysteries reveal themselves.

Using these three core principles as your guide, try making your way through the day and applying them to what you see all around you:

It's a study of experiences.
It's not what people think; it's how.
It's an observation, not an opinion.

Here is a simple exercise to get you started:

Watch a place or a setting you know intimately for a full hour. Write down what you see in detail. Not what you know, what you think or have opinions about, but what you actually see, hear, and even smell. It could easily be your local coffee shop that you know well but never directly observed with discipline. As you observe, think about these questions: What does it mean when people "have coffee"? How long does it last? What do people do when they're there? Are there patterns to how people meet, order, and settle in? Do they always drink coffee when they are "having coffee" with someone? What is the difference between "having coffee" and "having a drink"? (A lot, I suspect, but find out.) What happens when they disagree or disrupt these patterns? What are the rules that are unspoken but obvious to everyone? How do people move inside the space—the coffee shop, cafeteria, or café? What does the practice of standing in line mean? What happens when someone breaks the rules of who pays, or how loud to talk, or with whom to talk? A coffee shop is a complex place with rules, practices, and even a moral code. What matters is not what you think is happening; the only goal is to record the activity in front of you. Pay attention to the reality as it unfolds, not your assumptions about it.

Now try something even more challenging: observe a world that matters to you in your own life. The industry you work in has its own set of clear but undefined rules understood by most people in it, likely by you too. Try transcribing in a notebook the language people use as if you are hearing it for the first time. Professional speech is full of specialized terms and idioms that take time to understand and that make sense only to people inside that world. Write down these phrases and concepts and the meaningful differences that people use to make sense of their world. What do you always make time for, despite everything you say about your values and habits? When you walk into a meeting, which people do you see first? Last? Approach your daily life and its familiarity as a professional observer. Stop listening to what people say, and pay attention to how they organize themselves in space and in time.

With these building blocks of observation as your guide, you can pull the scrim off your everyday life. The routine of meetings, daily check-ins, or your relationships at home with family are wide open for your new observational approach. Again, set out to not make up your mind, but to watch and listen.

TRANSFORMING OBSERVATIONS INTO INSIGHT

These three principles of observation are a scaffold for us as we begin a deeper and more profound exploration of how observation works. What we are ultimately after are not just observations, but insights. An observation provides description, but an insight gives us pause. We all know the feeling: it's the flutter in your stomach when you can feel the presence of truth. Insights change what you see, hear, and perceive. They reveal new worlds to us. With a well-developed observational practice, we are better positioned to catch these fleeting but precious visions. In fact, without cultivating the skills of observation, it's impossible to even feel their presence. If we don't practice, we don't know how to pay attention to them.

What's the next step? If we want our observations to move beyond description to revelation, we'll have to up the stakes.

Most of us assume that we just open our eyes and "see" things. The best observers, however, demand that we explore this experience of "seeing" and "looking" with more rigor. This is the moment when we need to consider the background with more precision. How is it even possible that we look around the world and see, for example, not just an apple, but the world of an apple orchard, with trees, farmers, and apple pickers? We see not an isolated piece of MRI machinery, but a hospital with nurses, doctors, and technicians, hospital gowns and gloves. Not only do we understand what all these countless details mean, but we arrive at our understanding in an instant. Appreciating where insightful observation comes from requires that we go back to the origin story of observation itself. We need to understand what attention even is, and how seeing and perception work in the first place. This story does not begin with the science of vision. In fact, the human eye has very little to do with how and why great observations happen. Instead of corneas, lenses, rods, and cones, we need to spend time discussing the practical magic at work every day in our human perception.

PART ONE

· ·

THE FOUNDATION
OF THE PRACTICE

LEARNING TO SEE
OURSELVES SEEING

THE MAGIC OF PERCEPTION

I live on Thirteenth Street in the heart of New York City's historic Greenwich Village neighborhood. In Manhattan, the action happens on the streets, where walking is both a necessity and a pleasure. I do the same walk down Thirteenth Street several times a day—running errands, getting to the subway, and heading to the parks along the Hudson River. For this reason, Thirteenth Street has worn a deep groove of familiarity into my existence. I have been seeing the same sights for close to ten years now. But what exactly have I been seeing? How do I know what it means to look at Thirteenth Street? It turns out this walk on an ordinary Tuesday gives us an ideal illustration of our human perceptive experience at its most sophisticated.

When I leave my apartment to head west, I close the door to my building and position myself to walk down the block. In front of me, I see a blob of dark colors moving away from me. This blob is encased in undulating fabric, and it moves in erratic twists and turns. It stops and remains still for a moment until, suddenly, the fabric parts and I see human faces inside it. These faces huddle over a small white screen and erupt into laughter. Before I take any of this in, however, what I see is "fashion students." They are traveling in a pack with their stylish cocoon coats draping gracefully over their bodies. They are headed to a classroom at the Parsons School of Design, which is part of the New School, right down my block.

Just past these fashionistas, there is a beeping and the motion of something large approaching from behind. Without even registering a single detail—its shape, size, or make—I know it to be a delivery truck. A man leaves the truck running and hops out of the cab with urgency, leaping gracefully over the sidewalk's curb. He is carrying several boxes, and the truck's exhaust blows smoke into the air. What color is this truck? A muddy white or gray? Who knows. What matters for my perception is not a Pantone strip number shade of white or brown or gray. What I see is "truck color." By that, I mean I perceive it to be a truck, not because I register a particular color or material in the machine but because I see this hulking machine in the context of doing "truck things." I know what trucks do and what the delivery people hopping out of them do, and all this knowledge immediately snaps me into seeing the world of trucks. Because I know this world so well, I can predict most of the activity in it without any thought or analysis.

Now, only steps later, I notice bright orange cones, workers in vests, and the striped, fluorescent orange–striped barriers that line areas of the road. Instead of taking in all these details and perceiving them as separate elements—snap—I understand that it is a construction site. Around me are various pieces of equipment in different shapes and sizes, workers bustling to and fro, and mysterious markings all over the road. None of these pieces of information are relevant in isolation. In fact, I couldn't even describe the machines to you. I looked at them, but I didn't really see them. What I saw, instead, was the general human concept of a "construction site."

After I walk only a few steps more, the orange of the cones and the men in hats working are behind me, and I see a snarl of vehicles, scooters, and pedestrians in a clump toward the end of the block I am approaching. Moving shapes rush out of the cars to cross the street. There is a mess of erratic movement and pops of color as young people wave nonchalantly over their shoulders. Steam rises from the subway, and the flashes of color get obscured behind ribbons of hot air hitting the winter morning.

This mass of bundled lines and dots—all its complexity and chaotic movement—is filled with contradictory information. Young and old, frenetic energy and then silence. A vehicle arrives, and a child dressed in a rainbow of colors runs to the door and vanishes behind it. Two teenage girls move behind a delivery truck and disappear only to reemerge quickly on the other side. From the perspective of a driverless vehicle, all this activity is utterly incomprehensible. Objects appearing and disappearing are very difficult to predict without an understanding of their context.

From the human perspective, however, all this uncertain motion couldn't be more obvious. The chaotic running, the cars coming and going, scooters approaching and then departing, teenage girls appearing and then disappearing behind a truck. Even a toddler can find clarity in this chaos. It's just another day at "school."

The story of how we can do all of this—see not just orange triangles and squares but "construction site"—does not begin on Thirteenth Street. Instead, it starts more than a century ago at a Parisian café where a group of French philosophers first started to explore the idea of studying how we experience the world in its everyday magic. One philosopher in particular wondered whether it were possible to use a new kind of observational rigor to precisely describe an experience like walking down Thirteenth Street. How is it that we understand "school" and "construction site" and "truck"? How do we see these worlds of meaning and not the countless individual details that all of us encounter on a walk down any busy city street? This philosopher intuited that the answer to these questions would unlock the mystery at the heart of how humans pay attention to the world. His name was Maurice Merleau-Ponty.

One day in 1933, the philosophers Jean-Paul Sartre, Simone de Beauvoir, and their friend and colleague Raymond Aron were having drinks at a café on the rue du Montparnasse in Paris. Raymond Aron had just come from Germany, where he had heard a lecture by the philosopher Edmund Husserl. The German philosopher, Aron explained to his friends, was looking for a way to bring the everyday richness of life back into philosophical discourse. His concept, phenomenology, was about stripping away the abstractions of intellectual discourse from objects and experiences. Together with another German philosopher, perhaps the greatest of the twentieth century, Martin Heidegger, Husserl insisted his students put their attention back on "the thing itself." Aron picked up a drink of apricot liqueur sitting on their table and told them that phenomenology was the philosophy of something as ordinary as a cocktail. Rather than endlessly questioning whether we can ever really know what is the truth, this new philosophy focused on descriptions of how phenomena are experienced by us in our everyday lives.

Sartre and Beauvoir immediately wanted to learn more, so the story goes, and a philosophical movement began. Maurice Merleau-Ponty kept company with these writers and philosophers, all of them eventually dubbed "existentialists." While Beauvoir, Sartre, and many of their friends used phenomenology to explore questions like "What does it mean to be free?" and "How do we live authentically?" Merleau-Ponty asked a question that was much more original and yet startlingly obvious: "What does it mean to experience the world from inside a human *body*?"

Merleau-Ponty first asked this question in his book *Phenomenology of Perception*. He was a professor at the Sorbonne who used his academic connections to roam widely across disciplines that did not otherwise intersect—from philosophy to child development to cognitive psychology.

All these influences inspired Merleau-Ponty to call into question hundreds of years of how we think. Starting with Descartes, conventional wisdom conferred that making our way through the world was an intellectual pursuit. We stand detached, Descartes argued, observing and analyzing the world from inside our own minds. Merleau-Ponty's interests in child development and cognitive psychology inspired him to look carefully at how babies and young children perceive the world. As he observed the behavior of babies—first and foremost his own daughter—he could see that they were never detached or apart from their world. Quite the opposite, in fact. Infants existed in a kind of immersion in their world and didn't even perceive their bodies as separate from their caregivers. No one would ever suggest that intellectual and aware thinking—I think therefore I am—was an accurate description of an infant's existence. Why, then, should it apply to the rest to us?

Using the tools of phenomenology—back to directly describing the "thing itself"—Merleau-Ponty argued that the prevailing sensibility of all Western philosophy since Descartes was a bad description of how we perceive the world. Our bodies are not separated from the world; they are enmeshed in it. Just like babies, we exist in an immersive relationship with social context around us. Because we are both in the world and of it, he argued, the idea of mental maps or pure intellectual knowledge was false.

This radical premise—that we perceive the world at the most basic level from our bodies, not our minds—overturned hundreds of years of philosophical thought and tradition. And his phenomenology is still the most accurate philosophical grounding for understanding how we perceive the world.

You can experience his philosophical argument—perception is embodied, not intellectual—in optical illusions. Take a simple one, three straight lines in Müller-Lyer's optical illusion, as an example:

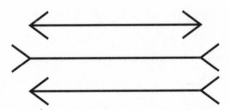

In the world of pure theoretical knowledge, a ruler measures these lines and they are always of equal length. Objectively, this is always true. However, in the world as we experience it, the lines are clearly unequal. We perceive not a field of vision with each line seen in isolation from the other, but a contextual understanding of all three lines in relationship. We take in both the figure and the ground, both background and the foreground. We see the whole of the image and not just the parts of three equal lines. The optical illusion tells us that the lines are not equal.

Is this true? In our experience, yes. Merleau-Ponty argued in his groundbreaking work that this is where reality exists: in our perception, not in the abstraction of the three equal lines on a ruler.

The same is true for our experience of seeing a train coming toward us from far away. You stand on a platform as the train approaches, and you see a small dot in the distance on the horizon. The dot doesn't change very much for a long time until—suddenly—it switches and the train becomes very large and close. This phenomenon isn't experienced as a steady recording of the actual size of the train, but rather the size is held constant in our experience before it quickly changes size from small to large. Merleau-Ponty called this "the size constancy phenomenon." In our experience, the size of the train—or truck or airplane—is held constant until it breaks down and gets a new size. The entire context switches at once, and the transition is abrupt rather than smooth. This is where our reality exists—*in our perception*.

Merleau-Ponty described his own experience of walking near water in a city. Far away he could see linear vertical lines that were murky and indecipherable. He took in these lines and shapes, but he could not "see" what was there. When he got closer, however, he understood that the linear vertical lines were the masts of boats. Suddenly the whole nautical world opened up for him. It snapped into place. After that snap, he couldn't return to seeing random lines on the horizon.

From this we can say that perception happens when it is in the context of things that have a meaning and a function in our lives. If you stand outside in the evening and listen to the sounds around you, it can be hard to hear if the noise comes from a party or a train passing by. But when that train horn blows, the party question disappears and you can fully imagine the scene of train cars, tracks, speed, and sound. It cannot be unheard, just as the boats, masts, and the nautical environment cannot be unseen. Think about what happens when you are trying to recall a song or a set of ideas. You struggle in frustration waiting for your memory to draw forth the recollection until—bam—the first line or just the bass line comes to you, delivering total recall, after which the entire song, melody, and lyrics snap back as a whole. How is it possible that assortments of what are really just colors, shapes, and sound waves can become our whole meaningful world—one we understand and know how to operate in? It is not a mystery, but it is breathtaking that we can all do it.

If the reality of our existence is in our perception—if it is in the rapid shift from a tiny dot to a huge train, or a series of lines that snaps into the world of harbor—what is this shift from whole to whole? And where did it come from? Before we can begin to see ourselves seeing, we must gain an awareness of how "wholes" exist in our perception.

Merleau-Ponty drew great inspiration for his ideas from a scientist and an artist. They each developed innovative work that helped him connect with a more accurate understanding of how to perceive the world. Through their art and science, the phenomenon of "wholes" earned its very own name. Today we know it better as gestalt.

THE FIRST LOOKING LAB

THE STORY OF GESTALT

1. THE SCIENTIST

The year: 1910. A thirty-year-old graduate student named Max Wertheimer hopped on a train in Vienna bound for the Rhineland in western Germany. Although well into adulthood, Wertheimer was feeling woefully behind in life's accomplishments. Surely it was time to grow up and get serious about his career as a psychologist and academic, but how? Though a bit brash, he had plenty of charm, good looks, and academic accolades. But he was still financially dependent on his family—his father in Prague was the one who paid for his train ticket—and, more urgently, he had no clear path for the next step in his research. Despite receiving honors in his experimental psychology projects—everything from letter recognition in patients with aphasia to the structures of logic that exist in legal psychology—Wertheimer still needed a topic for his "habilitation thesis," the advanced degree beyond a doctorate he needed to secure a university position. He could have followed many of his previously explored avenues, but Wertheimer wanted this next experiment to break the field of psychology wide open.

For inspiration, he opened one of his old notebooks written in his Gabelsberger, his self-created childhood shorthand. There he saw page after page of geometric figures and sketches. In many of them, he was trying to parse out when geometric figures that exist as parts become a whole. For example, when does the sketch of a rectangle with a sketch of a triangle on top of it become more than just a drawing of these separate parts? When we see these figures, when does our mind say *house*? And what is this "house-ness" that we perceive if it is not a rectangle and a triangle?

The more Wertheimer looked over his old notes, the clearer it became to him that he needed to devise an experiment to reveal this unassailable truth about human perception. What can science tell us about the magic of how we see the world?

Given the state of accepted psychological research at the time, Wertheimer knew it would be challenging to get funding or support from any of the establishment in the field. He had no interest in their labs anyway—he and others his age tended to see any experimental psychologist who started research before 1900 as stuck in the mechanical models of Isaac Newton. Max Wertheimer would need to create an entirely different kind of lab to understand how we perceive— not a rectangle and a triangle but a "house." He set out to create a Looking Lab.

Wertheimer was not wrong to be circumspect about the older generation working in the field of psychology in 1910. Although experimental psychology was a relatively young discipline, it was already in the calcifying grip of a German physiologist and philosopher named Wilhelm Wundt. In 1879, at the University of Leipzig, Wundt initiated the very first experiments in psychology, hoping to establish the discipline as a part of the natural sciences alongside biology and physiology. Like so many scientists of his time, Wundt was a reductionist: he wanted to break the mind down into discrete components he could classify and label. In his experiments, he set out to measure how sensations, or stimuli, created a response in the physical body. This was science, after all, and its role was to dismantle aspects of human consciousness into elementary parts that could be empirically measured.

He started with an investigation of the speed of mental processes. Mental process, he argued, could be broken down into constituent pieces and then timed with a stopwatch. In the inaugural experiment of his lab, Wundt arranged for his participants to observe a giant metal pendulum swinging back and forth. He measured the actual position of the pendulum swing and compared it with his participants' perception of the pendulum's location. The difference in these two numbers, he hypothesized, represented the speed of thought.

In his lab in Leipzig, which began with only a handful of graduate students and one room, Wundt created a powerhouse of doctoral researchers. In only ten years, he had gained significant funding from the German government and attracted the attention of two dozen doctoral students, several of them American, to come and conduct experiments under his guidance. What started out as a single room turned into an entire floor devoted to experiments of stimulus and response. One of these rooms was referred to ominously as the "reaction chamber": outfitted with electricity so that Wundt and his researchers could use an electromagnetic apparatus to create visual or auditory sense impressions for subjects and then measure reaction times in response to them.

Wundt and his students published their works of experimental psychology in a seven-volume, seven-hundred-page review entitled *Philosophische Studien*. Between 1875 and 1919, one hundred eighty-four PhD students came through the lab in Leipzig to study with Wundt, and his acolytes went on to universities and labs across the world—particularly in the United States and across Eastern Europe—to carry on his ideas about the nature of the mind and consciousness.

During his reign as the "father of psychology," however, pockets of intellectual rebellion began to emerge. Max Wertheimer felt fortunate to have landed in the refuge of one of these pockets, under the guidance of his mentor, philosopher Carl Stumpf. Stumpf had a love of hiking with good company. Walking with his mentor along mountain trails, Wertheimer found a sympathetic ear for his ideas about how to accurately observe human consciousness. The two researchers shared a common language through music. Stumpf had played the violin as a child, as well as five other instruments, and he had once thought of becoming a professional violinist. He used this understanding of music to guide his philosophical approach. What Stumpf heard when he experienced a violinist playing a succession of notes, for example, was not what was being studied in Wundt's lab in Leipzig. If a violinist changed all the notes but kept the same relationship between the notes, listeners would recognize the similarity between the two collections of chords. Stumpf knew that people did not perceive individual notes in isolation; they heard music in unified wholes. He started to incorporate more music into his academic work as he identified the tones and intervals that exist in all music. He called these musical elements "phenomena," and he linked his own work in musicology to that of the growing group of philosophers studying how we experience phenomena, or *phenomenology*.

When Wertheimer sought out Stumpf's counsel for worthy research subjects, the older philosopher guided him toward a special project he had been funding with his own money. It was a collection of the earliest recordings ever made of ancient song and music from across the globe. The recordings were captured using the technology of Edison's cylinder phonograms, and Stumpf was creating an archive to house them. Eventually the entire collection—ultimately encompassing around 150,000 sounds—was moved from Stumpf's research institution to Berlin's Academy of Music.

On free afternoons, Wertheimer would go to the archive and listen to its treasures. One of the collections he returned to again and again was the music of the Vedda singers, the people of Sri Lanka considered the island's aboriginal inhabitants before the sixth century BC. Ethnomusicologists had identified Vedda songs as some of the oldest lullabies in human history, often containing a three-part structure. The first part—sung to varying tunes and rhythms—was a resounding invitation to the fully awake child to transition to sleep. This was followed by a quieter section that beckoned the child to stay relaxed, and then, finally, a section of harmony to keep the baby sleeping.

At the time, the early twentieth century, other musicologists studying the music of the Vedda approached this "primitive" music as aesthetically inferior to European musical traditions. Wertheimer, on the other hand, wondered whether the music of these Vedda singers might be a key to unlocking the mysteries of consciousness he was chasing. In ancient Vedda songs, he discerned the same holistic integrity that he found in his own sketches of "houses" made from triangles and squares. The music might be simple, but it had strict rhythmic and melodic attributes; it had its own rules, variations, and motifs. In fact, in a paper he wrote, Wertheimer reasoned that even when its various parts changed, the Vedda music existed as a "whole."

Wertheimer's analysis of the music of the Vedda evoked the work of one of his professors, the philosopher Christian von Ehrenfels. In 1890, Ehrenfels used the examples of melody in music and argued that appreciation of it does not come from hearing single, isolated tones as Wundt would suggest. Instead, the melody is the melody only when the notes in succession are combined in a meaningful way. A melody can also be transposed into different scales—completely changing the individual elements—and yet it is still recognizable as the same melody. There is, Ehrenfels suggested, a Gestaltqualität that is present—something more than just the parts.

It was common at the time to say that the whole was the sum of its parts, but Ehrenfels's paper suggested something more radical: that the whole was *more* than the sum of its parts—the parts plus this gestalt quality. As Wertheimer worked his way through listening to the Vedda music, however, he felt driven to understand a notion that was so revolutionary he wasn't even certain how to articulate it. What if the whole was entirely different from its parts—not the sum of or even greater than the parts? What if the whole existed in our consciousness prior to the parts? And what if this whole actually determined what even counted as a part? Isn't it possible that we experience the whole first and then, later, fill in the parts? Is that what it means to see the reality of the world?

In developing his own Looking Lab, Wertheimer needed to prove that the Wundtian psychological approach and its reductionism were inaccurate. His experiments had to show that there was not a point-for-point correspondence between the physical characteristics of a stimulus—think of those electromagnetic tools in Wundt's lab in

Leipzig—and the psychological attributes of the resulting sensation. This, Wertheimer felt certain, was not how we experience the world. But how was he to show the existence of these "wholes," or Gestaltqualität, in an experiment?

Wertheimer's thoughts kept returning to an experience in which he knew he could achieve scientific accuracy: persistence of vision. For thousands of years, poets, artists, and philosophers had documented the phenomenon of the retina retaining images even after the stimulus had disappeared from the visual field. Aristotle wrote of the appearance of the sun even after he had turned away from the sky, and in AD 165 Ptolemy reflected on the colors in a potter's wheel that blur together and the distended light that seems to spill across the sky after a shooting star. More recently, groundbreaking experiments had been conducted in what was called "apparent motion" with another of Wertheimer's former professors in experimental psychology, Sigmund Exner. Exner asked his participants to look at two spatially separated and successive electrical sparks. He found that his participants could identify the sparks as two separate phenomena only when the intervals were longer than 0.045 second. When he shifted the experiment and moved his electrical sparks closer together, his participants reported an experience of movement like that of a strobe light with the spark moving from the first spot to the second spot. Following the teachings of Wundt, Exner concluded that the sensory phenomenon was accounted for merely by eye movements.

"But that isn't right," Wertheimer thought. The results did not occur because of eye movements. Something snapped into focus for Wertheimer. The results occurred, he realized, because of our dynamic perceptive process.

When the train conductor called out, "Frankfurt am Main,"

Wertheimer jumped up before he knew what he was doing. What he needed was a way to prove that the phenomena occurring in apparent motion had nothing to do with eye movements and everything to do with our perceptive apparatus—with the experience of motion occurring as a whole and determining the parts of sensation or stimulus. If he could find a way to measure this and scientifically capture the results, he might come closer to showing that the phenomenon of motion is a whole that we understand through our perception and not through our eyes.

When he got off the train, he headed immediately for the markets. He needed a tool that forced our size and motion constancy into stark relief. A zoetrope would do the trick. This popular children's toy contained an inner cylinder with a series of pictures on it and an outer cylinder with viewing slits carved into it. When children spun the inner cylinder and looked at the pictures through the viewing slits, they had the experience of seeing the pictures in continuous motion. Wertheimer had grown up with these toys and adored them as a child. In England, the London Stereoscopic and Photographic Company sold thousands of zoetrope—or wheel of life—models, and it was the first model Wertheimer found in the Frankfurt markets.

He ran with the toy to a hotel room and sat down on the bed. When he started to twirl the toy around in his hands, the slits in the tubes made the numerous images of a man bouncing a ball on his feet appear to move. Only seconds ago, the drawings were static, and now they appeared before him in dynamic movement. And yet, he thought with a growing excitement, they were clearly not moving in a scientific sense. In the context of Wundt's lab, these figures were static but he experienced them as moving. Here, before him, was an experiment that clearly demonstrated the inaccuracy of the constancy hypothesis, and it was all contained in a child's toy. Now he needed a way to prove that the motion was a phenomenon itself—occurring as a whole—and not simply the result of his eye movements.

Wertheimer was so excited by the possibility of experimenting with the zoetrope that he didn't even try to get back to Vienna or Berlin. Instead, he looked for a laboratory in Frankfurt. A former professor gave him space in his labs at the Frankfurt Academy and introduced Wertheimer to one of his most promising assistants, Wolfgang Köhler.

Like Wertheimer, Köhler was interested in both experimental psychology and physics. He immediately made a strong impression on Wertheimer, as he did with everyone he encountered. With his chiseled cheeks and high forehead, he commanded the room with handsome formality. Rumors spun about him, and students in Frankfurt speculated that he was a member of the nobility. Wertheimer was less interested in the gossip about Köhler's lineage than he was in his dedication to experimental psychology. Köhler trained as a physicist under the preeminent Max Planck and, like Wertheimer, received his PhD in 1909 from Carl Stumpf.

When they met, the two men immediately connected over their latest findings. Köhler had been working on acoustic experiments by placing a tiny mirror on his eardrum. In the reflection of this mirror, a light beam could record movements on his eardrum as it registered sounds. Wertheimer shared the notes he had been gathering for years regarding the existence of "wholes" in our perception. "I had a feeling that [his] work might transform psychology," Köhler wrote after meeting Wertheimer for the first time. "He observed important phenomena regardless of the fashions of the day and tried to discover what they meant."

Despite the energy of these first discussions, Wertheimer intuited that it wasn't yet time to share his hopes of a more rigorous experiment exploring apparent motion. The reason: he wanted Köhler to join him as one of his subject observers.

In early experimental psychology studies, it was not uncommon to enlist subjects who were also researchers, and the sample sizes were almost always small. This was because the phenomena the experimental psychologists were keen to isolate and test appeared spontaneously in each and every individual, regardless of their temperament or training. They were, quite simply, all aspects of being human.

Köhler immediately recognized in Wertheimer a kindred spirit, and he introduced him to another assistant at the university in Frankfurt, Kurt Koffka. Like Köhler and Wertheimer, Koffka studied under Stumpf and did his dissertation on imagery and thought. He had none of Wertheimer's compelling intellectual energy or Köhler's patrician charm, but Koffka was an industrious scientist and a productive writer.

With the intellectual strengths of the three men now combined into one collaborative conversation, Wertheimer knew it was time to begin his experiment. Although he first arrived at the university with a suitcase containing a primitive stroboscope, an instrument used to make cyclically moving objects appear to move more slowly or remain stationary, Wertheimer found access to an instrument that was far more versatile and useful for his purposes: a tachistoscope. Whereas the stroboscope presented continuously occurring stimuli, the tachistoscope could project a beam of light and then, with precise intervals of fractions of a second, interrupt the projection. Late in 1910, Wertheimer asked both Köhler and Koffka, as well as Koffka's wife, Mira Klein, to serve as observers in a mysterious experiment he was conducting.

Each one participated separately in one of the university rooms.

Wertheimer took out his tachistoscope and projected simple figures in front of his subjects: a line, or a curve, or the letters *a* or *b*. He found that if he flashed one figure—say, the letter *a*—and then waited an interval of about thirty milliseconds or less to flash the next figure, the letter *b*, his subjects reported that both *a* and *b* appeared present at the same time. When he made the interval longer between the projection of the two figures, on the other hand, two hundred milliseconds or more, his subjects reported that the two figures appeared to be flashing on and off in clear succession. When he found an interval somewhere in the middle, however, a time increment of around sixty milliseconds, his subjects perceived that one of the figures was moving from one position to the other. They stopped seeing the *a* and *b* as separate figures and instead saw only one of these figures in motion.

Wertheimer was fascinated by the presence of this phenomenon—of "pure movement" that connected the figures but bore no relation to any object in reality. His observers reported that they perceived motion without actually looking at anything. There was no figure being projected out of his tachistoscope. So what were they seeing?

Wertheimer called it "phi," using the Greek letter to symbolize the phenomenon. In his experiment, he noted the distinct presence of perception of motion without an objectively moving object. He decided to call this "pure phi."

In insisting on the existence of pure phi, Wertheimer was finally breaking away from Wundt and his acolytes. He had identified, in an elegant and rigorous experiment, that there was the presence of a phenomenon—"pure phi"—without any present stimuli. Motion existed in perception without an object moving.

The discovery was not groundbreaking—experimental psychologists had identified this occurrence in previous experiments. What was revolutionary about the apparent motion study was the cohesiveness of Wertheimer's analysis. He identified the presence of a whole: the phenomenon of motion before and even entirely separate from any actual moving object. It was a completely new, dynamic model of perception. With the introduction of "phi movement," Wertheimer ushered in an analysis of perception based partly on physiology. This is what it means to perceive—not as Descartes's abstract talking head, but from a body.

Wertheimer called Köhler and Koffka together to tell them about the results of his experiment. It changed everything for the three scientists who originated gestalt theory. As Kurt Koffka would later write in 1915, "[The wholes] are in no way less immediate than their parts; indeed one often apprehends a whole before anything regarding its parts is apprehended." Wertheimer could now effectively argue that our perception of the gestalt of pure phi motion precedes our perception of the letters a or b and even determines whether we register seeing them or not.

The reign of Wundt's reductionist approach to psychology was cracked wide open. It was nothing less than a new way of understanding the human consciousness.

2. THE ARTIST

That same year, halfway across Europe, Virginia Woolf attended an art exhibit at Grafton Galleries in London organized by her friend Roger Fry, and reflected upon it in her writing, "On or about December 1910, human character changed." The exhibit is now famously referred to as the birth of postimpressionism, and it was curated to introduce British audiences to the work of painters like Vincent van

Gogh and Paul Gauguin, as well as others, like Vanessa Bell, Virginia Woolf's sister. No other painter at the exhibit, however, was more responsible for shattering Virginia Woolf's understanding of human consciousness than Paul Cézanne.

Cézanne had died in 1906, four years before the exhibit, so he knew nothing of Wertheimer's apparent motion studies, but the two innovators were both chasing after a more accurate understanding of perception—one with the laboratory and the other with the canvas. As an artist, Cézanne did not suffer under the tyranny of Wundt's ideas about perception. He did, however, have his own aesthetic oppressors to combat.

I t was April 15, 1874, and a group of unruly avant-garde painters and sculptors were gathering at sculptor Gaspard Nadar's studio on the boulevard des Capucines in Paris. One of the painters, a dashing young man wearing fashionably cut pants from Paris's finest tailor, stood up to speak.

This was the moment, he challenged his fellow artists, to show up the jury at Paris's famed Salon. Almost everyone in the room had experienced rejection from the jury and its conventionally academic tastes. What the Salon wants, this young painter cried out in indignation, is mere accuracy and verisimilitude. The Salon wants only the clichés of the old masters, ever more versions of Ernest Meissonier.

The crowd of artists groaned. Not Meissonier again—everyone in the room had been subjected to the tyranny of this French classicist painter, the darling of the upper class, famous for his portraits of Napoleon and his military triumphs. The Salon is stuck in the past, the young painter called above the din of his fellow artists. Its jury is only invested in re-creating life as it has been seen before. We want life as it really is.

This painter, a short, brash young man by the name of Claude Monet, did not come from the upper classes. His father was a storekeeper and a merchant in Le Havre. Were it not for his obsession with painting, he wouldn't even be standing in this studio. He would be selling flour and grains from behind the counter of his father's shop. Instead, however, Monet was confident enough in his talents and obsessive ambition to eschew the Salon. Tonight, he and his fellow artists would show their work publicly for the first time, each piece in direct defiance of the Salon and its confining aesthetics. Monet wanted to capture not verisimilitude, but the ephemeral quality of light as it appears in our everyday lives.

In the room he was joined by artists like Pierre-Auguste Renoir, Alfred Sisley, Berthe Morisot, and Camille Pissarro. They called themselves the Société anonyme des artistes, peintres, sculpteurs, graveurs, etc. Only one of their cohort, Édouard Manet, had ever been accepted by the Salon—in 1873, for his more conventional painting *Le bon bock*. Everyone else was considered a maverick to the inside circle of the art world in Paris at the time.

Monet imagined that he was at the forefront of an entirely new movement in art: a way of painting that appeared unfinished to the conventional eye. In many ways, he was not wrong. The thirty artists on display that night were exploring entirely new ways of rendering reality in painting.

What Monet was only beginning to realize, however, was that there was another painter within their group who was far more radical, more modern, and ultimately more attuned to how we truly perceive the world around us. If Monet became associated with the movement of painting that pulled the art world away from the strictures of old masters and toward impressions of light's ephemerality, Paul Cézanne, the coarse and socially reclusive artist from Provence, was the painter who pushed art to its edge. This is because while Claude Monet's paintings showed us what seeing could be in our mind's eye, the art of Paul Cézanne forced us to acknowledge what seeing really is.

When the exhibit opened that first night back in 1874, the mainstream Parisian press mocked all the artists and their efforts. Satirist Louis Leroy, a critic for *Le Charivari*, poked fun at Monet's use of the word *impression* and described his work as akin to "wallpaper in its embryonic state." No artist, however, was as ruthlessly scorned as Cézanne. Critics and gallery visitors called his signature thick brushstrokes—les touches et les taches—the work of a madman. Édouard Manet, upon hearing that Pissarro had invited Cézanne to participate in the exhibit, removed his own work. He refused to show his paintings alongside Cézanne, an artist he described as a "bricklayer who paints with his trowel."

Unlike Manet, the other artists in the group viewed Cézanne as one of their own because they all were invested in capturing reality as it is experienced through light. Monet's water lilies, for example, show us the momentary effects of light and reflection on the water. In focusing on something as mundane as a pond flower—not an aristocratic lord or a historic battle—Monet and his fellow impressionists were showing the world that art exists all around us in our most everyday circumstances. The way to capture this reality, they argued, was through an attunement to how we see light.

This idea certainly created a radical break from the Salon, yet it still remained tethered to the philosophical conceits of the past. For this reason, even before the exhibit on April 15, Cézanne was growing increasingly frustrated with the impressionists. Monet's obsession with dapples of light was not so dissimilar to the work happening in Wundt's lab in Leipzig—fixations on reducing the whole of perception to sense impressions. Cézanne longed to capture something more permanent and essential about the world in his paintings. What is at the heart of what we see? he asked himself. Not just in a moment of light on the water but in the actual act of seeing. "You must think," he wrote, "the eye is not enough, it needs to think as well." Without ever meeting Max Wertheimer, Cézanne was asking the same questions in his own sketchbook. Do we actually perceive each and every dapple of light on the water? No. To insist otherwise is to be seduced by an intellectual conceit. It is akin to saying that we see the color, texture, or dapples of light on the chair instead of seeing, seemingly instantaneously, "chair." Cézanne wanted to do away with such misconceptions. He wanted to go beyond painting objects to painting the way we experience those objects.

While Monet continued to paint his landscapes in the town of Giverny—working through different parts of each painting in sections—Cézanne began to develop a radically different approach. First, before even beginning to paint, he studied his subject at great length. He learned to pay attention to the entire experience of it: "reading" his subject and understanding its essence. Then, after this period of sustained observation and attention, he worked to render on the canvas what he was seeing. These observations were not about reproduction or imitation. In this act of seeing, Cézanne argued, the painter inevitably brings in subjectivity. We are not cameras after all. "We should not be satisfied with strict reality," he told his friends. "The reforming process which a painter carries out as a result of his own personal way of seeing things gives a new interest to the depiction of nature. As a painter, he is revealing something which no one has ever seen before and translating it into the absolute concepts of painting."

When the April 15 exhibit closed a month later, it was considered, by almost all accounts, a failure. Although some of the artists sold works—Cézanne even sold one of his paintings—all of them owed money when they brought their canvases home. The Parisian critical establishment was not yet convinced of this new group's aesthetic imperative, and the fashionable set in Paris found the work of the impressionists unfocused and unfinished—sloppy, lazy, and, to some, just plain bad.

Paul Cézanne turned to his banker father back in Provence to dig himself out of his financial hole. Though his work was almost uniformly criticized, he didn't waver in his increasingly intense commitment to his vision. He found himself moving further away from any kind of depiction of three-dimensional depth. Monet and his fellow impressionists also rejected this three-dimensional point of view, but they still used a kind of superior perspective. The forms in their paintings—whether bridges, churches, or water lilies—appear blurry and difficult to see, as if they are in the far distance.

This superior perspective, seemingly in contrast to the three-dimensional approach so revered by the Salon and the old masters, was just as much of an intellectual fallacy. Like Wertheimer, Cézanne felt compelled to critique the same "constancy hypothesis" of a one-to-one relationship between sensory impressions and our understanding of them.

Think again about our perception of the incoming train on the tracks. If Cézanne were to render it, he could choose to paint either the small dot far away on the tracks or the switch to a train that is very large and close. If he were to paint a train between those two gestalts—a steady recording of the actual size of the train—he would not be an artist but a camera. His perspective—the human in the act of perceiving—was the reality. Without his subjectivity, the recording of the train would remain like the equal lines in the Müller-Lyer optical illusion. It would be a painting that was objectively true and yet, from a human experience, false. This—a painting composed of fakery, convention, and cliché—Paul Cézanne could not abide.

As his artistic vision grew more specific, he sought out new techniques to express it. He turned his attention to the landscape of his childhood home, Aix-en-Provence. In a complete break from Monet and the other impressionists, he did away with renderings of light altogether—shadows and light sources were completely ignored. The light, instead, is the same throughout these later paintings; it almost seems to come from within the objects themselves. Eventually, he let go of any attempt at illusion or naturalism. By the 1890s, he turned again and again to the Sainte-Victoire Mountain near his home, painting it more than sixty times. In each painting, he gives us a vision that is at the edge of incomprehensible. Just as Merleau-Ponty saw the lines and shapes on the horizon before arriving at the gestalt of "harbor," Cézanne gives us only the most nascent organization of lines and dots that snap into the experience of "mountain." We arrive at an understanding of the whole and then fill in the parts—whether they be light, color, or texture. The whole of "mountain," in fact, determines what counts as a part.

Although it would be decades before Max Wertheimer and his

collaborators would prove that the whole of motion exists in our perceptive apparatus, Cézanne was describing the same phenomenon: how we pay attention. While Monet and his contemporaries continued to paint an idea about light, Cézanne captured the way we fill in a part like light only after perceiving the whole. When we look at every one of his mountains, we experience a gestalt shift within ourselves. The magic happens in the moment between incoherence and "mountain." In this way, art moves from fakery on the canvas to an experience inside the body. We carry it with us every day.

Both Wertheimer and the paintings of Cézanne show us how to see human perception at work. And yet a scientist and an artist were not enough to change our culture's inherited but inaccurate description of perception. It took the philosophy of Merleau-Ponty to show us what it all means. How do we make meaning from what we see? When does the world cohere for us and why? How do we see other people?

In his work, Merleau-Ponty sets the stage with our perception of gestalts and uses this framework to call attention to how we make our way through the world. The traditional philosophers of his day were arguing that seeing was about perceiving the parts of sense-data. This data consisted of discrete bits of raw data that were then processed by our retina or eardrum. The experience of seeing a chair began with processing the color, light, shape, size, and width of the object in front of us. Then, only after all of that was accomplished, could we ultimately arrive at the understanding of a chair.

Merleau-Ponty grew impatient with this description. He argued that this was simply a bad description of how we arrive at an understanding of a chair. As much as he was bothered by this approach, however, there was another camp of philosophers that aggrieved him even more: they described the process of seeing as sensory data entering the mind and then getting processed into categories. If you see a chair, you already have "chairs" placed in categories of space, time, and perhaps even furniture. Therefore the sense-data goes into a kind of algorithmic sausage factory—if this, then that—with categories growing more and more granular until reduced to the most likely category left: a chair.

Early movements of artificial intelligence in the 1960s and '70s used these philosophical conceits of categories of thought to program robot prototypes. A robot reaches out an arm to touch an object it perceives. What is the object? Take in data points—height, shape, and color. Use these data points to match up with a preset category—furniture—and then use that category to reduce possibilities until arriving at the most likely outcome: chairs.

Merleau-Ponty understood that although both philosophical camps had useful ideas about the mechanisms of sight, they revealed nothing about our human experience of perception. What we actually see is not a direct reflection of what is in the world of reality around us. Perception happens inside us; we change what we see to reflect who and where we are in the world. We inhabit a world of meaning, he tells us, rather than exist in a world made up of meaningless sense impressions. This meaning exists everywhere all around us: at our dinner tables, in the steel, concrete, and wood of our buildings, inside our offices and schools and across all of our streets. It's not in categories or data points but in wholes. And we cannot "see" it because it is right under our noses. Just like the infants he studied, all of us experience the world from inside it.

Isn't it more accurate, he argued, to say that all of us understand what things are and what meaning they have through our shared social context? We know that chairs are often placed around tables, so if we see a dining room table with objects around it, we tend to assume these are "chairs." Chairs are for sitting and they are connected to the worlds of tables, meetings, dinners, reading, writing, and many others. They have meaning to us, and that *meaning* is the first thing we see when we see a chair. Of course, he concedes, we also take in raw sensory data through our retina, eardrums, and other sense organs. And maybe if we lived in a culture that never used chairs, we would have to go through something more akin to a natural science process of observation. But this is rare. We see a chair in front of us because we know what chairs are for. We *perceive* meaningful gestalts—or organized wholes—not meaningless empty data in parts.

And isn't it extraordinary, he asked, that we can pay attention to parts without losing our sense of their whole—that we can analyze the figure without ever losing awareness of the ground? He takes on some of his most iconic predecessors, philosophers like Immanuel Kant and David Hume, and uses the practice of phenomenology to argue that they have been getting attention and perception all wrong. When I carry a glass, how do I know how to put it down on a table? When I see a triangle, why do I see a triangle and not a collection of lines and then a triangle? When I hear a song, why do I hear the melody of it and not sound waves and single chords? In our experience of perception, Merleau-Ponty observed, the whole or the sum arrives before the parts and determines which parts we perceive. We see a dish of steaming hot tamales on the table of a family, for example, and understand that it holds meaning as a Christmas dish. We can pay attention to details like the smell of the pork and the sight of the hot chili peppers, but these details are not discrete and unrelated. Instead, they serve to enrich our empathic understanding of the entire social world: It is Christmas, and the family is celebrating with a meal together. The tamales are part of a background practice of holidays and celebrating and Grandma telling stories and the smell of wood on the fire. This is what makes our attention and perception extraordinary: we can study details at all scales and still hold on to the whole, the gestalt that gives each context its coherence.

One of Merleau-Ponty's favorite thought exercises to ponder was the wonder of looking through a keyhole. First, human perception can understand its relationship to the world as it exists through that tiny hole in the door. Our perception allows us to see inside the hidden world and to understand it spatially as a place of vastness despite the constrictions of the keyhole. And then, miraculously, we are able to immediately shift back into our experience of life in a full-size body. This artful flexibility of attention is nothing less than magic. And it helps all of us to appreciate the sophistication of how we pay attention to the world.

It is an attention that is involved, not detached. We are not looking down at the world as if through the lens of a microscope or the window of a lab but looking through it, within it, from inside it. It was this philosophical breakthrough that synthesized both the scientific rigor of the gestalt theorists with the artistic clarity of Cézanne's approach. There is no "world" and "us"; there is only us from inside the world.

Merleau-Ponty's arguments about perception broke the philosophical world wide open. When we bring a greater awareness to how we see ourselves seeing, it gives us our first experience of what he is describing. We humans move through a world of shared meaning, and these "wholes," or gestalts, make up the immersive fabric of our social contexts.

Because phrases like *worlds* and *social knowledge* can sound so vague in the abstract, I'm always looking for ways to encounter a heightened awareness of these perceptive gestalts. Fortunately for all of us, there are masterful visual artists who can immerse us in an experience of Merleau-Ponty's philosophy in three-dimensional time and space. Although not many of us have access to labs replete with tachistoscopes or dozens of paintings exploring the same mountain in the South of France, every one of us can go out and see ourselves seeing. It turns out there are Looking Labs all around us. We simply need to go out and find them.

THREE ARTISTS

How to See Beyond
Convention and Cliché

My alarm went off at 4:00 a.m. in my hotel room in Austin, Texas. I had approximately one hour to get myself out of bed and off to the campus of the University of Texas. There, on the rooftop of the university's gleaming new student activity center, was a work by the light artist James Turrell. The installation, called *The Color Inside*, was deceptively simple. It was a small white building with an opening for a door and slatted wood seating lining the three sides of the interior. Instead of a roof, however, Turrell constructed an oculus—a circular viewing window—that brought the experience of the sky into direct contact with the visitors. The art was not the building or the shape of the oculus: Turrell had no frame or any focal point per se. He asked me to immerse myself in the experience of the light, but this was only his initial invitation. At its core, his work forced me to bring awareness to my perception. And it is this awareness that is the foundation of all the greatest observations.

I arrived at the oculus when the world felt heavy with humidity and dark—not yet 5:00 a.m. and long before sunrise. I took my spot on the wood bench inside the structure and let my head lean back against the wall. From there, I settled in and looked upward. In this position, I could see the dark sky through the oculus. As I looked up, the room felt as if the sky had been pulled down to form the ceiling. The stars against the dark night felt very close, almost like a painting. But I experienced other light in the room as well. Turrell was subtly adjusting the colors that appeared around the oculus through a carefully considered lighting design. Time passed. The dark purple of night was surrendering itself into . . . what? A strained yellow? The light around the oculus shifted as well. Was the sky turning orange? Around the oval of the oculus, new colors started to form before my eyes. It was an experience of motion, but I wasn't moving. What was happening?

Through the oculus, the sky felt as if it were closing in on my body, almost as if it were pressing down. But then a bird flew across the oculus. Everything suddenly changed, and I perceived the sky as very far away.

These shifts were the same "gestalts" that Wertheimer investigated in his Looking Lab in Frankfurt. Unlike experiments that happened over a century earlier, however, Turrell's Skyspace is inviting us into a modern-day laboratory of perception. When we look up through his oculus, our brain perceives a whole and then fills in the missing or ambiguous visual information with our own maps of the world. As I perceived motion from the bird, my nervous system did not register the stimuli as a bit of discrete data. Instead, my perceptual experience shifted immediately from one whole—the sky is as close as the ceiling—to another whole: the sky is far away.

I stepped outside Turrell's small viewing structure to experience the dawn as I would normally see it—and feel it. This "dawn" reassured me with its familiarity; its gauze of pink and yellow hues was just what I expected. I could stop the exhausting process of *seeing* and shift back into an autopilot of perception. This is the way we tend to experience our daily lives—in these habitual grooves of familiarity. Oh, that's right: "dawn." As soon as I stepped back into Turrell's oculus installation, however, my entire body was thrust into confusion. It certainly wasn't any understanding of dawn that I had experienced before. It prompted me to ask myself: What is the convention of "dawn" and what is the reality of "dawn"? By manipulating the viewing through the oculus with something as simple as LED lights, Turrell changed the entire context of what I know of as sky.

Although James Turrell started making his light installations in Los Angeles in the 1960s, his interest in perception began as a student. While studying perceptual psychology at Pomona College, he discovered Merleau-Ponty's *Phenomenology of Perception,* and it captured his imagination. Turrell was a California-born Quaker and a conscientious objector to the Vietnam War who found a kinship with this Left Bank academic and writer. This is because Merleau-Ponty understood that what we see is not a direct reflection of what is in the world of reality around us. Perception does not just happen inside us; we change what we see to reflect who and where we are in the world.

Turrell's use of light and color in the Skyspace thrusts me into an embodied exploration of Merleau-Ponty's philosophy. Without perception, there is no such thing as color. Light waves are colorless until the moment they hit our bodies through our eyes and brain. A Pantone strip with a particular color red will be completely different when that red is on a Ferrari versus the American flag. And yet, if the Pantone strip is the same, why do we experience these reds in such profoundly different ways?

Look around the room where you are sitting right now. Pay attention to how you experience the colors you see. Have you ever considered the fact that your initial assumptions about color are not just conventional but patently false? If we want to gain a more accurate description of our encounters with color, we must move beyond easy clichés like the sky is blue or the grass is green. We need to test our own perception in process.

Fortunately, I knew exactly which artist could enable this type of Looking Lab.

When I arranged to meet Seth Cameron to experience his paintings in person, I did not make my way to a painting atelier or a high-ceilinged loft. Instead, I rang the buzzer at a space that until recently had been the home of a much-loved Manhattan institution, the Children's Museum of the Arts. In addition to being an acclaimed New York–based artist, Seth is also a highly regarded art educator: in 2020, he was appointed executive director of CMA. As we walked through the moving boxes and dismantled exhibits of over a decade of children's joyful experimentation in the arts, Seth explained that the museum was moving a few blocks away with a renewed focus on partnerships with neighboring arts organizations. In his new role, Seth has even more of a chance to explore his ideas about the role of art in our lives:

What constitutes art and how do we experience it? And should arts education focus on teaching ideas and techniques, or should it help children to discover the everyday art that's present in their perceptions of the world? Maybe arts education is no more than the philosophical unveiling of experience—observing the presence of the hurly-burly and celebrating it.

One of Seth's areas of exploration—in both his work as an artist and an arts educator—is how we experience color. This interest might have started with his mother. He told me she was a kindergarten teacher, so her role was to introduce young students to colors. "But she showed them color by bringing out the color wheel: *This is green and this is red*," he said. "That's not color; that's just naming things. Arbitrary names on a wheel give an equivalency to colors that is not accurate to our experience. We think of red as equivalent to blue, but that is not true. Our eyes aren't built that way."

Seth's manner is thoughtful and unassuming, but when our conversation shifts to the philosophy of art, his cadence takes on a new intensity. It angers him that abstractions like the color wheel keep children, and all of us, from fully appreciating our everyday experience of art. I told him about my visit to James Turrell's Skyspace, and he nodded his head in appreciation.

"Turrell is part of a long tradition of artists who are reacting against the culture of the image," Seth shared. "People don't know how to look at paintings because they think they're looking at images. We have that relationship to things on the wall anyway because it's a relationship to abstraction. What's interesting about painting is that we don't think of it as an illusionistic space, but anything on that wall is an illusion. We see space whether we want to or not. Unless they are artists, most people still stand right in front of a painting even if it is an abstract work. Why do they do that? There is no image there."

While the two of us talked, Seth guided me past dark rooms and cardboard moving boxes into a dim space that once served as the museum's lobby. Here he had hung one of his own watercolor paintings on the wall. This was ultimately the reason for my visit. I wanted to connect the dots between James Turrell's exploration of light and Seth's sensitivity to color. Before I could even appreciate the color in the painting, however, I noted how both of our bodies oriented to the frame on the wall as soon as we approached the painting. Without saying a word, we both situated ourselves in the best possible positions to perceive what was before our eyes. Side by side, we stood to face the painting in front of us—intuitively and silently we lined up about six feet from the frame.

Merleau-Ponty called this orientation of the body "optimal grip," and Seth reminded me that though our bodies shift in relation to any work of art, one painting in particular playfully accentuates how and why this happens: *Las meninas*, by the great seventeenth-century Spanish painter Diego Velázquez, is like a mathematical puzzle. There are several different perspectives within the painting, but there is only one place to stand that reveals to the viewer what exactly is in the painting's mirror.

Seth cited it as one of the greatest examples of Merleau-Ponty's articulation of the optimal grip. It is a painting that tells you where to stand. "Your body is a part of the experience," he said. "You can watch people go into the Prado Museum in Madrid to see it and, without knowing what they're doing, they shift to a certain distance away. If you do the geometry to find the exact spot where you can see the image in the mirror, you'll find that people are already standing there. Their brains have already figured it out."

As my own body adjusted to appreciate Seth's painting, I saw what appeared to be a rectangle with a block of a purple color on it. Seth walked me through the exact construction of what I was seeing.

"It is entirely symmetrical and orthogonal," he explained, "and it is a double square, a two-to-one ratio, and roughly related to the size of the body. It is painting as a mirror. But that is also part of the control mechanism telling you where to be."

I could feel the optimal grip in my shoulders. My body was situating itself to perceive the colors before me. For that's what was there to experience: Seth's work was nothing but color in a framed rectangle. When I first approached and took it in, the color appeared to be a kind of purple. Not a color wheel purple—an abstract conceit of a cartoon collection of grapes—but a kind of murky purple that felt thick with nascent shapes. It was the purple of waking up just before sunrise and feeling one's way through the dark.

As we both stood and experienced the art, the colors began to change. A green horizontal rectangle at the center of the painting became more apparent. The sense of purple receded. Around the border of the painting, a blue emerged. These experiences were happening to both of us at the same time. The shapes and colors were not memories or ideas we each held about what this or that color might represent. Instead, our experience was a physical response. Though I was standing in a building in downtown New York, I was also back in the world of Wertheimer's apparent motion study. Just as we all experience the phi of motion, we also all observe the way the colors and shapes emerge and recede in Seth's work in the exact same way.

For Seth, this experience is where art happens. It is the revelation of color and shape that happens over time when we pay attention. Our actual experience of color is available to all of us, and it has nothing to do with a color wheel. It is certainly neither the image nor the narrative of what the painting represents.

"The process is simple," he told me. "It's watercolor paper mounted to a panel. The water releases the pigment on the paper, and it soaks in. When the water goes away, you have no binding agent. Unlike oil or acrylic painting, practices where the binding sits up on the surface, there are no brushstrokes, no surface in watercolors."

For Seth, this lack of surface allows each viewer's experience of color to be the art. By removing the biography and the story behind the work—there is no linear interpretation about which stroke came first or which section was completed last—the piece serves as a portal. What is inside the frame is an invitation to all of us to see something emerge. This rectangle of color before me started to feel akin to the wild yeast starters I use in my own kitchen to make sourdough bread: it is a catalyst for a phenomenon to occur.

"Normally when you're working on a painting, you carry the image with you in your mind," Seth said. "But this series of paintings didn't make mental images. These are just experiences. I would be working all day in the studio on this and then turn the lights off and realize I had no memory of my work. There was no image in my mind of what I had done that day. I had to return the next day and look at the piece and wait the same amount of time each day to have the experience of my eyes readjusting and switching back."

Seth pointed to a color in the center of the painting. "There is an implied blue square there made up in four quadrants," he said. "But if we left and let our eyes look at something yellow and came back in, for ten seconds that blue square wouldn't be there.

"Our eyes only start to see it after ten seconds. Every single time we look at this work, we always have to wait ten seconds to see the blue square."

I find it fascinating that all of us—me, Seth, you, everyone—have to wait the same ten seconds to see the blue square. His art reveals an experience that is true for all of us. It is not subjective; it is not objective. It is a truth in our shared space of experience. And just like Wertheimer's work in his Looking Labs, Seth's work reveals a path forward for all of us to escape the color wheel models of truth. Great observation begins and ends with seeing beyond convention to the actual experience before you. *"To the thing itself . . . "*

James Turrell and Seth Cameron show us how to gain access to a more authentic experience of light and color. But there is an aspect of our everyday human experience that goes even more unexamined. How do we perceive space? What if art is not even the object at all but the space that exists around it? How can we bring more attention to this space, and what would it look like to see it unfolding before us? These are the questions driving Merleau-Ponty when he asks what we experience walking into a room or carrying a drink to the table. One artist understood how to ask these questions with unprecedented precision. Curators and art historians called him a minimalist because his work used a limited repertoire of objects, like cubes and blocks. It was a term he found onerous because he described his work as not minimal at all, but "simple expression of complex thought." His name was Donald Judd, and his art changed the way all of us perceive our own bodies in space.

Judd was born in a small town in Missouri in 1928 to a modest midwestern family. He served as an engineer in the US Army throughout the 1940s, and it was only during this time that he began to rigorously explore drawing and drafting architectural shapes. In the 1950s, he turned his focus toward philosophy at Columbia University while also painting at the Art Students League of New York. Like other artists of his generation, including James Turrell, Judd grew frustrated with the limitations of painting as a medium: It was too constricting for his goals. He did not want a representation of life—the parlor tricks of old-world European paintings like *Las meninas* with their abstract renderings of perspective. He wanted to break away from painting altogether. Instead of representing space on the canvas, he wondered, could art create a more direct experience of space in real time? How do we experience our bodies through space?

My first breakthrough with Judd's work happened at the iconic Glass House of Philip Johnson, in New Canaan, Connecticut. Along with many other lovers of architecture and design, I toured his 1949 house to experience his approach to geometry and proportion. With the vast proportion of the house constructed out of glass, the walls offered a porousness: between the glass and the landscape, there was no "inside" and "outside." When the house was built, Johnson famously quipped that he had "very expensive wallpaper."

I was walking toward the house and reflecting on its transparency when something caught my eye. It was clearly a piece of art but, as a concrete cylinder stuck in the ground, it seemed to belong more to the world of a construction site. When I approached it, I saw it as a two-dimensional object. I moved toward it, however, and something profound happened. In my attempt to achieve optimal grip, the piece snapped into the third dimension, and I was suddenly looking at space stretching out into a plane that opened in front of me. It was as if Judd had opened a door, a magic portal of perception, invisible and yet present, there for anyone willing to take the time to see it.

I stepped back—I was in the second dimension again. Step forward—

three dimensions. Step back—only two. The more time I spent with the piece, moving around its sphere, the more I could appreciate the precision of this shift.

The snap of the gestalt was constructed to occur not in feet or inches but in millimeters. The smooth surface of the cement refused to distract me from questions about meaning—it wasn't trying to look like a body or a bird or any other kind of representation. Instead, the piece

existed to reveal a singular experience: gestalt shifts. Judd had meticulously crafted the shape of the cylinder to reveal itself to me at
specific points of orientation.

Back and forth I stepped, seeking out optimal grip and rocking
between dimensions. It left me feeling unexpectedly optimistic—this
seemingly simple piece of concrete that amplified my depth perception. My encounter with Judd's work *Untitled* (1971)—the first of his
larger freestanding concrete objects—was so provocative, so akin to
Merleau-Ponty's exploration of our perception that I had to find out
more. I immediately set out to experience Judd's work at Dia Beacon,
a contemporary art museum an hour north of New York City. There
I stood before Judd's pieces *Untitled* (1975) and *Untitled* (1991).

In both works, plywood boxes project out into space from their
wall mountings. They are arranged according to simple lines and
grids, so it is impossible to interpret any one box as more important
than another. Although the material here is plywood rather than concrete, the effect of two dimensions breaking open into three was the
same when I approached. I moved my body back and forth and in
different directions to perceive the objects. Where was the optimal
grip? Maybe it didn't exist. Or maybe my quest to look for it was the
point of the art. Is it possible that Judd was directly influenced by
Merleau-Ponty's philosophy? I set out on a pilgrimage to find out.

If you want to get to Marfa, a tiny town in the high plains of the
Chihuahuan Desert in the western part of Texas, you need to set
aside significant time and a reserve of patience. The town is three hours
from the nearest airport in El Paso and at least half a dozen hours
away by car from larger cities like Austin and San Antonio. In 1979,

Judd came here in search of a different way to create art. He was disenchanted with the power brokers of New York's 1970s art world, the curators and agents who were taking art away from the studios and transforming it into commerce on the walls of galleries and auction houses. Judd longed for what he felt was a more authentic experience of art and art making.

"Most art is fragile and some should be placed and never moved again," Judd later wrote in an introduction to his work. "Somewhere a portion of contemporary art has to exist as an example of what the art and its context were meant to be. Somewhere, just as the platinum iridium meter guarantees the tape measure, a strict measure must exist for the art of this time and place."

Marfa's vast open sky, low-lying horizon lines, and moody brown and purple moonscape was just that "somewhere." Judd bought 340 acres that included the abandoned army buildings of Fort D. A. Russell. Within the vastness of this space, he created more than fifteen different outdoor pieces and one hundred different aluminum works housed in the former artillery sheds. By 1986, Judd's partnership with the Dia Art Foundation led to the creation of the Chinati Foundation, a nonprofit arts organization dedicated to Judd's work in Marfa as well as that of some of his contemporaries, including the light installation artist Dan Flavin.

Marfa was precisely where I landed after a long drive through the scruffy brown Davis Mountains on a late summer day in 2020. Several decades after Judd's initial vision, Marfa has become an arts mecca with dozens of restaurants, food trucks, an art house bookstore, and a glamping site replete with high-end shampoos and bodywash. All of this in a town of less than two thousand full-time residents. Marfa's most photographed work of art is an elegant white box of a store with the word PRADA blazoned across it—not a single other store or structure in sight on a stretch of lonely road toward the high plains of the Chihuahuan Desert.

It would be easy to assume that Donald Judd's art would be forgotten in the hype. And yet, when I approached his fifteen giant concrete structures installed one after another upon the land, I had to stop and take a breath. The structures, each about eight by eight by sixteen feet wide, cannot be experienced without their context—a messy desert field of scrub brush, succulents, and, on some days, even snakes. This is not pure art here—a precious piece that can be stripped of its context and placed on a pedestal in a museum. Judd's giant concrete boxes are in the landscape and of it, meticulously placed in lines and rows, inviting me with a challenge: pay attention to how you are perceiving these.

Because attention is the ultimate goal here. It is Donald Judd's challenge to all of us. How do we look at these pieces? Where do we stand to find any coherent whole? How do our bodies move in relationship to them? How do we see the space between each of them?

I moved myself closer to the pieces, and my body wanted to line them up, to find an optimal grip where their placement gave me a unified frame through which to see the landscape on the other side. I found the exact spot and felt a sense of relief at looking through the concrete boxes to a single image on the other side. Then a group of people walked past my frame and the gestalt shifted. Just as in James Turrell's Skyspace, Judd's piece was forcing me to move from a framed image of the desert landscape to a moving image of people walking in the distance.

As I wandered around the concrete boxes, I longed to see the pieces from above, to arrive at a perceptual coherence that felt entirely organized. And yet Judd does not allow for such an experience. It's no coincidence that the Chinati Foundation won't permit drones to take aerial photographs of these structures. This work is meant to be "seen"

by humans in time and space. Directing a computerized camera to capture images from above is completely beside the point. It removes us—and our bodies—from the experience.

As I moved in and around these simple concrete structures, there was no one place to stand, no ideal alignment. The experience left me feeling unexpectedly unmoored. Was this dislocation Judd's artistic interpretation of Merleau-Ponty's philosophy?

After I made my way through the concrete blocks, I moved to Judd's compound, what he referred to as "the Block." These buildings included a room holding a large section of Judd's library. It was there that I gained a better sense of the source code of my experience. In all his deceptively simple structures, Donald Judd's library, writing, and notes reveal that he was inspired by the philosophy of Merleau-Ponty. I discovered that while Judd was a student at Columbia, he wrote his thesis on Plato. In it, he wrangled with Plato's focus on true knowledge: the idea that abstract, theoretical knowledge exists apart from the messy reality of our experience in the world. It's clear in even this early writing that Judd is bothered by this notion. Just as we cannot strip works of art from their creation, he argued, we cannot perceive universal truths without acknowledging their context.

In this way, with beauty and elegance, Donald Judd responds to the optical illusions that the gestalt theorists once pondered. The concrete cylinder at Philip Johnson's Glass House, for example, parallels the experience of seeing the famous duck and rabbit illusion: you can shift back and forth between dimensions—two dimensions into three or a duck versus a rabbit—but you cannot see both at the same time. Through these pieces, he disagrees with Plato: There is no platonic ideal, no universal truth. Instead, the only truth is contextual. One minute the truth is a rabbit and the next it is duck. In order to understand a figure, you have to consider it against its ground. To know a person, you must understand them within their world.

And, as in Judd's art, you never actually "see" these concrete shapes apart from their world on the high desert plain. In an essay written in 1964, Donald Judd succinctly articulates his vision, "The thing, as a whole, its quality as a whole, is what is interesting."

Whether it is the sky as seen through Turrell's Skyspace, the color purple that morphs into greens, blues, and yellows in Seth's watercolors, or the feeling of seeing space unfold in fifteen concrete boxes in a desert, all three of these artists' works show us that the truth of our perception is far stranger and more interesting than common assumptions would have us believe. Looking Labs abound—through apparent motion studies, the hills of Provence, and in the dusty scrub of western Texas, each one of them asking us to question what we see.

How can you connect with a more accurate experience of your perception in daily life? Think back to what it was like taking a picture of a landscape at sunset with a film camera. For those of you who have never used one, the color of sunsets has a yellow tint on the resulting negative or developed photo. This yellow tint was "objective" reality—a value-neutral reality of an optical device capturing traveling light waves. The human experience, however, contained none of this tint. Our perception held the color constant; we saw the sunset as simply "the sunset"—color correcting without even realizing it. Today's digital cameras have their own function, called "white balance," which does a similar color correction. But the example of the analog camera helps to illustrate how a technical recording of the objective world is different from the world we experience. This is where reality exists—in our perception.

Artists are uniquely sensitive to this fact, but all of us can learn from their gifts. Go out and find a Looking Lab—or even better, make one of your own. Get away from your screens, turn off your notifications, go out into the wilds of reality, and look around. Let go of all filters—clichés, conventions, color corrections, whatever they may be. Try to pay attention to the simple act of seeing. "To the thing itself." What will appear before you?

WHAT IS ATTENTION?

Spend sixty seconds right now and just experience your body in space. Think about the book or reading device in your hands, the sounds outside, the feeling of your legs on the seat or the couch. What do you feel against your skin? What can you hear? What you are experiencing right now—whether it is how your hand understands where to turn the pages of this book or how your body creates just a bit of distance from the person next to you on the train—reveals some of our perception at its most profound. This is how we pay attention to the world.

Consider the example of a rose. A gardener, an interior designer, and a suitor getting ready for a date all pay attention to a rose in completely different ways. The gardener sees the rose in the world of plants and flowers, and she uses her knowledge of soils, fertilizers, pruning, and pest prevention to care for it and prepare for its bloom. The interior designer looks at a rose and pays attention to the ways it will appear on a console in a crystal vase and whether its height and color will complement the gold of the antique mirror he just put on display. The suitor getting ready for a date looks at the rose and wonders whether it is the right flower for the night: Will it signify loyalty and ardor or overzealous enthusiasm?

The rose is in all these worlds, and we pay attention to it in very different ways. A scientist—a botanist, for example—can also observe the rose and focus on aspects of its properties, studying the presence of microscopic fungi on its petals. This way of paying attention— focusing in with a scientific lens—is valid and useful to modern life. But Merleau-Ponty argues that the focus of a scientist—an intellectual approach—is not as basic to our knowledge as our social understanding of the rose. The traditions of philosophy have misled all of us about this for hundreds of years. Attention is not an intellectual experience. Science might tell us something about the rose, but it will never reveal our relationship to the rose. What does the rose mean to us in our world?

The metaphor of lighting design can help me make this feel more concrete. A designer chooses different types of light for different objectives: a focused light, for example, is good for tasks like sewing with a needle or reading a book. This light—often a spotlight—provides a good description for the conventional understanding of how attention works. Everything inside the light is of importance, while the world that exists beyond the light is irrelevant. Paying attention in this conventional sense is about concentrating only on the spotlight. The scientist puts a spotlight of focus on the rose and pays attention only to what is in the circle of light.

Merleau-Ponty argues, however, that our primary experience of attention is like another kind of light that designers and architects use. This one is ambient, and it fills the room with a more diffuse light.

With ambient light—more like a floodlight—the background and the foreground are both relevant. When we walk into a room, we ignore this ambient light just as we ignore the floor underneath our feet. It's so obvious, it's not even worthy of notice.

Ambient light, or the floodlight, is how our attention works most of the time on an ordinary day. Because it is so obvious, it doesn't feel natural for us to be analytical about it. It's not even in our general awareness. We move through the world, down the street, past our friends and neighbors, driving or biking, walking or sitting. Merleau-Ponty was the first to suggest that this happens in a kind of viscosity—an enmeshed existence in the world around us. Yet when we are deliberate and careful with our descriptions of everyday attention, we realize that the floodlight is all around us all of the time.

So much of our current cultural conversation around attention refers to our experience of the spotlight focusing in and tuning everything else out. When as children we learn to read a sentence, for example, or we look through a microscope at a slide of bacteria, we are aware of our attention concentrating on the spotlight. What we miss understanding with this fixation, however, is that we are always, first and foremost, paying attention with the ambient light. In fact, there is no such thing as looking or focusing without a broader attention on the context.

Don't believe me? Imagine a white dot. Now imagine that same white dot on a page of white paper. It's imperceptible. We can only ever make meaning of the white dot—we can only see it clearly—when we perceive it within the context of its background.

All of this is to say that there is no spotlight of attention without the floodlight. Even an astronomer looking through a telescope, or a software engineer working on a line of code is making meaning of their work through this broader form of attention on their social world.

Social world, hurly-burly, background, our act of *being* in the world: philosophers and thinkers use these kinds of phrases because they are trying to describe an experience that is right under our noses. Attention is both too close to see and too far away to analyze. For most of us most of the time, our attention to the world is invisible to us. German film director Wim Wenders named one of his most acclaimed movies after this experience of familiarity: *In weiter Ferne, so nah.* Attention is faraway, so close.

If all this still sounds vague to you, let me bring up some examples of the floodlight of attention that everyone has encountered. Think about a brilliant soccer player moving the ball down the field. If you watch them at their best, they are not giving their undivided attention to the ball; in fact, they focus on nothing in particular. The best athletes seem to see space and movement in real time and can project into the near future, all at once. Soccer players have patterns of movement they practice with drills, but in the moment such patterns become like the training wheels on a bicycle. They withdraw into the background. In their place is a glaze of attention: a focus on the entire phenomenal field. It is as if they can see all the players' movements and the curve of the traveling ball in slow motion against the backdrop of the entire field.

What's more, when soccer players are interviewed after a match, they rarely have anything specific to say about what they just did, even when what they did was something extraordinary involving extreme skill and virtuosity. They have no conscious awareness of it. These players are rarely excellent public speakers, but it is remarkable how little they have to say about events that happened just moments ago. This is because such moments were not experienced as awake and fully in front of a transparent consciousness. Often, they need to see the footage after the match to even understand what happened.

A great basketball player can toss the ball over his shoulder and sink a shot without ever looking at the hoop. Two dozen ballerinas can move around a small stage without ever bumping into one another. An Olympic swimmer knows exactly where the competitor's body is in relation to her own even though it is a lane away and five strokes behind. How do they do this? This has nothing to do with the spotlight and everything to do with the slowing down of our perception. A floodlight of attention on both foreground and background: everything and nothing. This is an accurate description of how we experience attention in intellectual pursuits as well—going over spreadsheets, for example, or writing an email. Yes, we are focusing on tasks, but we are able to concentrate in this way only because our broader attention understands the meaning: the greater context of the desk where we are sitting and the computer keyboard we are typing on, not to mention the meaning of abstract concepts like "human resources," "customer service," and "budget allocation."

Our attention is an unheralded miracle of flexibility: it has an ability to contract and to expand, to appreciate the relevance of details as well as to comprehend the vastness of worlds. Attention can make meaningful play with patterns, scales, narratives, movements, and myths. When we start celebrating attention's ultimate capabilities—instead of relegating it to the mere subset of focus and concentration—we come that much closer to our goal of mastering observational skill. Learning to observe life's hurly-burly requires an understanding of how to pay attention.

To give you an example of what this kind of attention looks like,

I sought out one of the world's greatest observers. He has cultivated a mastery of the floodlight's glaze of attention. Although he is well versed in the latest scientific research exploring vision—everything from ophthalmology, neuro-ophthalmology, to vision therapy and neurophysiology—his area of expertise has nothing to do with seeing. His name is Gil Ash and he is considered by many to be the most influential and experienced sporting clay, skeet, and trapshooting coach in the world today.

I first met Gil on a ranch in the middle of Montana, where he was conducting one of his highly regarded coaching sessions in clay shooting. Gil, a sturdy Texan from Houston who drops dry asides about the intelligence of geese, is widely regarded as this highly specialized sport's greatest innovator.

The game of clay shooting was created in the nineteenth century when gambling on shots of captive birds like pigeons and grouse started to offend people. Sport shooters sought out a mechanical way to replicate the flight patterns and trajectories of birds they found in the wild. By the turn of the twentieth century, self-loading traps with clay targets were being used. The first iteration of clay targets, terra-cotta, proved too hard to consistently crack open with a shotgun's bullet. By the mid-1950s, however, trapshooting manufacturers turned to a softer clay for its traps, and the increase in shooting success led to more popularity and the sport's permanent placement in the Olympic Games. During his over five decades, Gil's dedication to technical precision in shooting has revealed new possibilities for the sport. He and his coaching team are dedicated to studying how the brain sees the clay get released from the trap and what happens in the milliseconds before the body executes the shot.

At our session in Montana, I watched as one of the shooters in the workshop loaded his shotgun and stood at a distance from the automated trap machine. Gil called out, "Pull," and a small, orange-colored disk was hurled from the machine and traveled across the sky at one of many precisely determined trajectories—each one a different height and speed. Most beginners lifting their shotgun to shoot the clay miss altogether—it seems to be traveling at incomprehensible speed. The barrel of their gun follows their eyes as they try to track the clay across the sky—too slow, too late. For a beginner, it's almost impossible to shoot anywhere but at the disc because we have been pointing at objects we are also looking at our entire lives. This act of pointing at what we are looking at is essentially automatic, out of habit, so if the targets remained still, beginner shooters would improve quickly. But the target is moving, requiring the shooter to track the clay with their vision and point the gun ahead of the clay, ensuring that the shot cloud and the clay arrive at the same spot at the same time. Added to the demands of this task is the fact that the shooter must keep their primary vision on the target at thirty-three yards and point the gun barrel which is only thirty-three inches in front of their nose.

"The situation is complex," Gil explained to me. "Your eyes are seeing one point at thirty-three inches, the end of the gun's barrel. They also need to consider another point: the clay disk at thirty-three yards away. How is your perception going to coordinate those two data points?"

Although the clay disk was pulled at different angles and different speeds, Gil told me that the most crucial factor in learning to pay attention to the disk is the relationship between the object flying and its background. If the background is far away, the disk flying on it is experienced as slower. If the background is closer to the shooter, however, the disk appears to be moving faster.

"The perceived speed is less important than the background," Gil told me. "Within three seconds you need to react to the depth, width, and size of the space along with the speed and movement of the disk. It is a four- or even five-dimensional space of vectors and speed."

Given this complexity, there was no way to bring an intellectual awareness to the act of shooting. Here in Gil's broken clay targets was even more evidence that Merleau-Ponty's description of perception and attention was correct. Instead of thinking through a shot, trying to analytically process all the variables, Gil coaches his clients to train their bodies to slow down perception.

"A high disk, like a high bird"—Gil pointed up to the target moving across the sky—"is experienced as going up and down with a sharper movement than a low disk. That makes the low disk feel slower, even if it is actually pulled at a higher velocity."

To help explain this description, Gil Ash shared an insight that could have come straight from Max Wertheimer: "Speed is relative to the background, and it has very little to do with what your retina sees."

It turns out the sport of clay shooting, the quintessential act of looking down the barrel of a gun, has very little to do with vision science. Instead, it is a game won through a mastery of how we experience our vision—a game of highly skilled perception. In fact, as his vision weakens with age, Gil relies on the strength of his eyesight less and less. Vision loss doesn't hinder his ability to engage with the sport at a masterful level.

"Neuroscience research has proven that it is the relationship between your near and your far sight that matters, not the strength of your overall vision. I don't need a young person's eyes to see. I just need to feel it and to see the relationship between the disk and the background. These days, I don't even need to look at the disk to know if one of my clients will hit it. I just know."

Gil's knowing gives us another inkling of what it looks like to systematically observe the background. In his lifelong study of the sport, he is using a kind of second-order observation—the process of hyper-reflection—to improve his skills of perception. He is not applying a scientist's focus to his efforts—he never loses the whole gestalt of the clay moving across the sky. Instead, he slows his body down to gain better information about how the disk is traveling. In his coaching, he teaches his clients to "lose their minds," to get out of their heads and let their bodies speak.

"If you don't let go of the fear of missing," he told me, "you will be pretty awful at this sport. The subconscious mind is much faster to react. The aware mind, the conscious and analytical approach, is the one to watch out for. If you think you can't hit the target, you won't."

It is through the relationship between background and foreground, nearsightedness and farsightedness, the barrel of a gun and the tiny dot of a clay far off in the sky that Gil Ash pays attention in his sport. Even in this seemingly simple set of constraints—gun, lead, clay, machine—there is a tremendous amount of complexity. His glaze of attention gives him a way of processing all these variables—not seeing but perceiving—and the shot cloud from his gun smashes the clay target wide open almost every time.

If Gil's mastery of clay shooting gives us an illustration of how to observe the background and its relationship with the foreground, how can we apply that to a context that is infinitely more complex, one involving a social world? How do we bring all this newfound awareness of perception to the task of observing other humans against the whole hurly-burly of human action? In this first section, we explored opportunities for you to see yourself seeing. The technical precision I outlined will serve you well as you turn your observational practice out toward the world of other people—their societies, cultures, beliefs, and behaviors. If a context of guns, lead, clay, and machines creates a vast complexity, the social world of humans ups that complexity level many orders of magnitude. In part 2, we will explore how to approach observing the human world with greater richness and depth.

Before moving on toward direct application of Merleau-Ponty's philosophy, I want to leave you with this concise primer for your everyday observations. For each of these six common misunderstandings about human perceptions, Merleau-Ponty offers all of us a way to bring more rigor and precision to how we look at the world. I encourage you to cut this out or keep it near you when you are ready to begin observing more complex phenomena. Let his philosophy serve as your vaccine against the easy answers and trendy ideas that infect so many of our contemporary conversations.

PART ONE PRIMER

Six Common Misunderstandings about How We See the World

MISUNDERSTANDING #1:
WE HEAR AND SEE RAW DATA

I would argue that there are two significant ways we misunderstand and underestimate how humans perceive the world. At the most basic level, we think seeing is about receiving and processing data from the world. Our senses see, hear, smell, taste, and touch the world around us. Our brains then process myriad data, and, somehow, we experience the world we live in as meaningful and as a place we know how to operate within. What we experience when we see or hear, then, according to this first assumption, is the causal product of atomic sensations. We can see the parts without the whole. By *atomic*, I mean discrete and meaningless data like light or sound waves with no reference to the human world. In an atomistic view, properties are independent of each other. The color blue is not dependent on the blue sweater we see it on. Objects are what they are because of their intrinsic nature, gaining only superficial features from whatever relationship they happen to enter into. This is the realm of raw sense-data. We hear sound waves that can be measured in hertz and smell an odor or scent in our olfactory nerves. What else would it be? this common assumption leads us to ask.

But how do we immediately recognize the smell of burning bread or a forest after it rains? Naturally, we smell ozone and other chemicals, but we experience it as burnt toast or wet wood. Merleau-Ponty and other famous philosophers like William James claim that we never experience meaningless raw sensations. They exist in nature but never in our experience. Sense-data is always experienced as part of a human and meaningful world. There is no such thing as a figure without a ground. The whole defines what counts as a part. There are cases where we can't place a smell or a sound, but they are rare.

MISUNDERSTANDING #2:
SCIENCE EXPLAINS IT ALL

The other major misunderstanding has to do with how we humans perceive other humans. In my professional life and among my students, I often hear people explain a complicated phenomenon or human activity by saying things like, "That is just human nature." In the cognitive and experimental psychology tradition, human activity is researched by conducting experiments on graduate students and extracting simple laws of human behavior. Lately, words like *bias* are supposed to explain everything about why and how we make bad decisions that aren't rational or even decent. These ideas have been some of the main ways of understanding human behavior for the last decade. We, humans, are explained by simple frameworks like "fast" and "slow" thinking, where fast is irrational (bad), and slow is like natural scientists (good). It is a simplistic framework that provides easy answers to explain the complexity of human nature.

Another trendy idea is that all human behavior can be explained by evolution. Love, sex, having children, and wanting to be promoted are just the results of evolutionary biology and they can be fully explained within this tidy framework.

Even more exciting is the idea that studying our brains with new technologies like fMRI scanners helps us get to the bottom of why we do what we do. We are our brains, and descriptions of how the frontal cortex and the amygdala light up when presented with stimuli like images and sounds give us a clear narrative to follow. We can build new products, create political messaging, and optimize dating services based solely on scans of the brain.

In economics, the market and financial activity can be described in mathematical models based on the assumptions that humans react to incentives and companies want to optimize profits. In other groups of more left-leaning economists and political scientists, all human history can be understood through the lens of oppression. Everything that is wrong in the world can be reduced to one word: *capitalism.*

Lately, a new scientific narrative of human nature has emerged. Large language models and AI claim they can predict what we think and want to write, and can even create our movie scripts. Why? Because: AI.

These theories poorly explain the experiences of fundamental phenomena or concepts of the human world such as attention, care, and perception. Merleau-Ponty's philosophy shows us that these simplistic ideas are cop-outs for actually trying to explain phenomena that are more complicated, nonlinear, and beautiful. For our purposes, we could call those lazy concepts *reductionism* or sometimes even *scientism*. If we want to get humans right, we need to challenge ideologies like these.

In his philosophy, Merleau-Ponty helps us acknowledge that we always operate, first and foremost, in a social world, sometimes in several worlds simultaneously. *World* sounds like a technical term, but we intuitively understand it. Think about the "world of theater" or "the world of high finance." They have, as the German philosopher Martin Heidegger famously said, shared structure. All worlds have equipment people use. The world of theater has tickets, stages, actors, scripts, theatergoers, and budgets. The world of birthday parties involves balloons, cakes, guests, and candles. People use those pieces of equipment *in order to* reach specific but often unspoken goals, and the people in the world have reasons for their behavior that are tied up with our complex identities as actors, parents, or bankers. We live in those worlds and are so familiar with them that we rarely think about how they work or what the rules are. We give ourselves an identity by picking up practices in these worlds. We are beings *in* and *not outside of* the world. Simple frameworks do not explain our worlds and practices. They are *wholes* that involve skill and mastery that can't be taken apart by conducting reductionist experiments or brain scans. There are good reasons why it is challenging for AI technologies to know which world we are in when we talk, discuss, or do anything meaningful. Neither generalized artificial intelligence nor economic modeling has come close to understanding or operationalizing the problem of worlds. And scientism or reductionism isn't helpful if we want to truly observe and understand. Instead of lazily accepting the account of cognitive psychology, neuroscience, or even physiology, we need to go back to the phenomenon. Phenomenology is trying to put us in touch with a direct account of the phenomenon of perception without giving a psychological or causal account. We need to watch and listen without easy answers.

MISUNDERSTANDING #3:
WE SEE LIKE A CAMERA

A camera can register data about whatever you point its lens at; it can record and reproduce the exact color, shape, size, and distance, just like a sound wave recorder can register the precise frequencies around us. It feels intuitive that we would perceive the world in the same way as a camera—the idea that humans also absorb sense-data and reproduce it as if we are taking a picture of what we see.

But it is a mistake to think that we see like a camera or hear like a sound wave recorder. It is also wrong to believe that a camera is better at seeing than a human. A camera is undoubtedly superior to humans if seeing is about absorbing sense-data and reproducing it accurately. But what a camera doesn't do is see a world saturated with meaning, and it doesn't describe the world as we move through it and involve ourselves with it.

It is a common misunderstanding to think that what we see and hear when we walk down the street is raw data hitting our sense organs. It is counterintuitive that primary sensory input (such as color, sound, movement, distance, and numbers) is not what we see. These inputs are not perceived in the way sense organs receive the sense-data.

We should distinguish between raw sense-data as it is received by our sense organs and how we experience sense-data in the human world of meaningful objects, color, space, distance, etc. We do not perceive our experiences as a machine would, as a detached recording of the world around us. Humans are always already in the human world, and what we see is perceived as such.

MISUNDERSTANDING #4:
PERCEPTION IS INTELLECTUAL

We are our brains, right? It is the brain that controls everything, and our eyes are hardwired into the brain. Surely, we see with our conscious minds—or so we assume. We can explain our actions by studying what we think. The history of philosophy is full of versions of this idea. The empiricist philosopher John Locke suggested that all perception and attention really is sense-data reaching our body. That data somehow adds up to our experiences in the world. Rationalists like Immanuel Kant took this idea further by claiming that the sense-data that reaches our eyes and ears is organized in categories. We have concepts in our brain, and the data is separated by a mental mechanism that makes the data part of our experience. Merleau-Ponty calls these two positions "prejudices": both have a stronghold on how we explain what perception is. He collapses empiricism and rationalism into one category he calls intellectualism. His argument is that experience is happening in a prelinguistic and preconceptual manner. Most of the time we understand the world without language, and we have no propositional relationship to the world: We are not inferring or believing anything. We simply operate without intellectually processing anything. We are not minds, brains, or consciousness. We are what we do, rarely what we think.

MISUNDERSTANDING #5:
SEEING IS SUBJECTIVE

Another common assumption is that our experiences are ours and ours alone. When we hear, feel, or see something, it happens within us in a way that feels private. We can also have thoughts that belong only to us. No, says Merleau-Ponty and existential phenomenology in general. Our every thought, every word, and all our experiences are happening on a social background we share with others. There is no way to have any thoughts without having them as part of a shared human world. In other words, there is no way to think, feel, or experience anything without doing it on the background. Even the most abstract concepts like numbers or string theory are always understood on the background of the world they belong to—quantum physics, for example. Martin Heidegger's word for this idea in his strange and often impenetrable language is *woraufhin*. It can be translated to something like "that on the basis of which." All thoughts and concepts are parasitic on a background of what he calls *familiarity*. In a way, this is Heidegger's most important insight. The hurly-burly is familiarity. It is *that on the basis of which* everything is understood. We know what we are familiar with, and we know that others know. Merleau-Ponty refers to this attitude as empty heads turned toward the world.

MISUNDERSTANDING #6:
ATTENTION IS FOCUS

When we get worried about our children doing their homework or try to teach them how to use a fly-fishing rod, we tell them to "pay attention." When we drift off in a daydream during working hours, we attempt to "focus" and direct our attention back to the screen or stove we are supposed to be looking at. Most of us feel distracted by social media and the onslaught of emails we need to respond to. Paying attention, then, we assume, is zooming in on each of these individual things. Attention is awareness of only one activity or goal and the ability to remove all distractions from that one goal.

While that is certainly one important way of thinking about attention, Merleau-Ponty wants to convince us that there is a much more basic and important way to talk about attention. He believes that our general orientation toward a world with which we are deeply familiar is a more basic and primordial type of attention. Attention is how I walk down the street with a general glaze: I am focused on everything without focusing in on anything. Without putting it into language, I know what streets are and I can skillfully navigate the highly complex task of walking or driving down them without anyone getting hurt. Our perception and attention are not obscure phenomena that are impossible to describe or observe. Human perception and our ability to observe is astounding but not impenetrable. What is important is that we can look at and see the structure of that general glaze of attention. We can study and observe how we are familiar with the world. The working title of this book was *How to Pay Attention*— although it turned out there was a better and simpler one. The point is that we can learn to observe and analyze how other people pay attention to the world. That is the meta-skill Merleau-Ponty calls hyper-reflection.

PART TWO

· ·

GETTING STARTED

THE GREAT EXCAVATION

BEGINNING WITH CLEAN OBSERVATION

t is just before 7:00 p.m., and the students are starting to file into the auditorium where I'm holding our first class of Human Observation at the New School. They wander in—philosophy majors, design students hopping over from Parsons School of Design, engineers, musicians, performers, doctoral candidates in religion, and user-experience designers, all of them curious about this class with the odd, old-fashioned title. Despite their various reasons for enrolling, most of them have one thing in common: they are naturally curious about the world and eager for an education that will show them how to make sense of it.

Before we can even begin, however, the students need to dig themselves out from under the dusty layers of calcified thinking. I liken it to the great excavation. We need to scrape away clichés, conventional thinking, dogma, and any other theoretical layer that is clouding their ability to directly observe the world. It usually reveals itself in ex-changes that sound something like this:

> **ME:** New York City is a good place to observe human beings engaged in social practices. It's a pressure cooker of a place.
>
> **STUDENT #1:** Don't you mean New York City is the ideal example of a place to observe human beings being exploited by corporate America and toxic capitalism?
>
> **ME:** Well, no. Actually, I don't mean that at all.
>
> **STUDENT #1:** But observing anyone in New York City is inevitably observing an economic system of income inequality that is growing at a faster rate than at any other time in America since the Gilded Age.
>
> **ME:** I don't want to start any observation with a sweeping statement about income inequality. You might be right, but I want to begin a discussion of observation using an actual observation.

Let's try that again.

> **ME:** Really, at its core, this is a class about perception and attention. How do we pay attention without the interference of assumptions and prejudices?
>
> **STUDENT #2:** By assumptions and prejudices, I assume you are talking about the liberal media bias.
>
> **ME:** This course is trying to get at something even deeper and more profound than human bias. We are not looking at what people think but how.

STUDENT #2: What is deeper and more profound than the biases of the institutions giving us our information about the world?

ME: You draw a conclusion in what you ask, but we are not concluding right now. We are just doing clean observation. Looking and listening for a change. We don't yet know if your conclusion is true in any given context. We haven't verified anything yet.

STUDENT #2: There is no clean observation. Everything goes back to whether we are being spoon-fed propaganda about governmental overreach.

ME: Does it though? Does *everything*?

Okay—take three:

ME: When we want to understand human behavior—take romance, dating, and coupling as an example. We need to begin with observation.

STUDENT #3: Romance and dating have become completely secondary to self-actualization for people today.

ME: How so?

STUDENT #3: Just look at Maslow's Hierarchy of Needs. People are seeking out enlightenment more than they are seeking out old-fashioned conceits of marriage and courtship.

ME: I am familiar with Maslow's Hierarchy of Needs, but I am much more interested in hearing about something that you have actually observed.

STUDENT #3: I just think people are getting tired of the Tinder swipe culture. Everyone is swiping for new soulmates in some endless quest to achieve enlightenment. Now that we don't have to struggle for food or shelter, everyone is obsessed with achieving the top of Maslow's pyramid.

ME: Did one of your interview subjects actually say that to you?

STUDENT #3: No one has to say that. It's just how everyone in my generation feels.

And now from the back row:

ME: Throughout the course, you will go out and begin your own observation practice. You will carefully observe a small number of individuals and their social context.

STUDENT #4: Why would we start with a sample size of only two or three? I can get a sample size of two billion people on Facebook. We don't need to look; machines do that for us.

ME: You can get data on two billion people. But what are you actually observing?

STUDENT #4: It doesn't matter what I'm observing. The data is the data. If millions of people are doing it, the scale should speak for itself.

ME: But what is the scale? What does it mean?

STUDENT #4: With sample sizes that large, machine learning algorithms can tell me what it means. It's beyond my human eye to see.

ME: What is wrong with having a look for yourself? Our human eye, the powers of our human observation, are uniquely well suited to discerning meaning and understanding changes in culture. We need to use large data sets to validate if what you observe is true, but only after having observed carefully to figure out where to start. We are here to honor the skill and practice it more.

As you have probably guessed, the excavation process involves digging up these young minds, dusting them off, and exposing them to the real world of lived experiences. Many of today's students begin with a prepackaged and preconceived framework about how to begin observing. This is often because that is what they have been taught to do. These frameworks are the lenses through which they perceive all phenomena in the word. Such boilerplate frameworks run the gamut from extreme left to extreme right: identity politics, Marxist theory, entrepreneurial free market and libertarianism, and everything in between. It is not their fault, really—today's students have been taught not to think (look and listen) but to opine. And now, because of constant affirmation from social media, they are experts at passing out broad, sweeping abstract ideas to explain human behavior.

Unfortunately for them, none of these frameworks are of any use if we intend to study experiences. Instead of finding data points to fit a preconceived story, we need to seek out a genuine understanding of the context. Only then can we form an opinion or theory.

So together in the auditorium, we begin the painstaking process of developing analytical thinking skills. For those who like instant traction and snappy conclusions, this process is challenging. Unmoored from comforting bromides and left without a clear sense of what they perceive, the students come to feel exposed and raw. Now we can begin the good old-fashioned hard work of actually observing the world around us.

There is absolutely nothing wrong with searching widely and across a variety of disciplines and data points for a better understanding of human behavior. The excavation process is necessary only when this understanding begins and ends with tidy abstract frameworks or with sample sizes in the millions and billions—"big data" analyzed by machine learning algorithms.

And if you think that my students have ready-made answers that cloud direct observation, you should spend time with the people who work in corporate America or large siloed public sector organizations. I've reviewed hundreds of strategic plans for some of the world's largest corporations and public institutions, and the ideological frameworks are often identical. Whether it is a beverage company, a producer of building materials, or a global health care initiative, the structure, language, key analysis, evidence, arguments, recommendations— even the typeface of the graphs—are often exactly the same. All of us, in organizations big and small, can benefit from a great excavation.

Once we get this process underway, we are well positioned to do clean observation. Now it's time to choose a phenomenon to observe.

When we are starting out, any human phenomenon will do. New York City is filled with humans doing interesting things, and I am certain your city or town is as well. I encourage you, just as I encourage my students, to start out learning to observe with something seemingly simple or banal. We are just beginning our practice, so it's more than enough to observe how bodies move around in space and perceive their everyday worlds. Take your inspiration from Merleau-Ponty and carefully observe people walking down the street, entering a room holding a drink, or moving around a kitchen while cooking. From these first simple observations, start building an awareness of the background—or the hurly-burly—into your practice. To get you going, here are just a few ideas my students explored. You'll quickly find your own just by observing your own street, neighborhood, school, or office.

THE EXPERIENCE OF STANDING
AND TALKING IN GROUPS

Try to observe a room with many people talking—a conference, say, or a cocktail party—and look at the bodies trying to coordinate the appropriate distance to stand from each other. My student saw bodies constantly adjusting to land in the shared optimal distance. A group of four people needs to adjust when a new person arrives. They shift to a comfortable position for all of the five people now standing in the group.

People will also adjust the volume of their voices as the standing distance changes. All of the members of the group will grow louder or softer, moving inches back and forth from one another, to make themselves and others comfortable. Most of the time, they are not even aware of these constant adjustments, but it is possible, and revealing, to observe the movement.

Now see if you can do these types of observations in a context where people are from different cultures: At a gathering in a bar for the World Cup, say, or an outdoor market with food from all over the world. People from some cultures like to be relatively far from those they talk to, while others like to be up close; some people speak more softly, while others prefer to express with volume and enthusiasm. If you can visit an international gathering with people from different worlds, try to observe how the different styles coordinate with one other, attuning to one another below the threshold of consciousness. Often people from cultures that are more comfortable standing farther apart will end up with their backs against the wall as people who like to be closer creep into their space. This dance of distance and volume can be hilarious to observe, but it also gives us helpful information about modulating our own distance and volume.

THE EXPERIENCE OF MOVING
AROUND AN ART MUSEUM

In the nineteenth century, European and American museums were often created as temples to visual art, with Greek columns and monumental stairs to climb. The Metropolitan Museum of Art in New York City or the British Museum in London are both examples of a magisterial approach to showcasing art. Today, however, museum directors and architects are moving toward democratizing art by building museums that are more like a marketplace or a mall, where people can engage with the art on their own terms. LACMA, the Los Angeles County Museum of Art, is an excellent example of this new kind of people's art museum. There the idea is that a more direct human relationship with art can replace the outdated reverence and awe that nineteenth-century architecture fostered.

One of my students directly observed people at a museum and noted what changed between the bodies, the artwork, and the space. You can do this as well at a museum in your city. Stand in a corner of an art museum displaying paintings, sculptures, or any other fine art. Twenty years ago, museumgoers would move around the room trying to get close enough and at just the right angle to take in the artwork. These bodies were seeking out Merleau-Ponty's optimal grip while also attuning to an appropriate cultural distance for viewing the art. This unconscious dance was commonplace at art museums all over the world.

Today, if you take the time to stand in the same museums, you will see a very different scene. The art, the room, and the number of people are the same, but the dance is completely different. The bodies are no longer trying to get in the correct position to appreciate the art. In fact, art is no longer the central theme of the museum. My student saw that the primary organizing principle of museums is no longer physical: it's digital. The bodies in the room are not trying to get in the perfect position to experience the art; rather, they're putting their bodies in place for others to see them experiencing the art. This is not because of a new layout or design changes; it is because of the cameras on our mobile phones. When you ask people why they visit the museum, they say, "I want to take something home with me. I want to create memories." Their visit is no longer about appreciating art; it is about the memories made through their documentation of the visit. Optimal grip is achieved around the camera lens, not around experiencing the art itself.

THE EXPERIENCE OF SLEEPING ON THE STREETS

Most big American cities today struggle with a population experiencing homelessness. Sleeping in the streets shouldn't be a part of any affluent society, and we struggle to understand what to do about it.

One of my students chose "sleeping in the streets" as a phenomenon to study. He went out for several long observation sessions between the hours of midnight and 4:00 a.m. When out, he observed either people who chose not to sleep in a homeless shelter or people who did not make it to the shelter before it closed its doors at 9:00 p.m.

The first observation my student noted was *light*. City streets at night are not dark; intense, bright streetlights light them up. As it turns out, the light is a good thing because sleeping in the darkness is dangerous. People huddle around the brightest spots in the streets to stay safe. Light keeps people safe from the danger of others on the street, particularly people behaving erratically.

The next realization he noted was the *sound*. While the rest of us sleep, the city is busy building, cleaning with giant hoses, and picking up garbage. It is filled with the loud noises of driving, dragging, pushing, and drilling.

The last observation he had was the *smell*. Because of garbage removal with old food fermenting for days in garbage bags, the odor is intense. My student described it as the smell of tooth decay, the same smell dead bodies have when they have been left undiscovered for too long. The intensity of these three sensory experiences—bright light, roaring sounds, and the smell of decay—might help explain why people sleeping on the streets get very little sleep.

If you start this kind of observation process with indignation, anger, or hubris—using the lens of anti-capitalism, or social justice, or libertarianism—you are beginning with ideology, not observation. That means it's time to go home and try another night. Remember, you are looking for clean, direct observation: Your opinion based on received wisdom is not the point. You are not looking for someone to blame or a solution to fix what you are seeing—that can come later. First take a look. See what you can learn about what you see.

Starting with careful observation about the phenomenon will prepare you better for arriving at useful insights about what to do. If you start by reading dozens of think pieces or reaching for theoretical frameworks, you skip the essential foundation for understanding. All that data gathering will come in good time. But first, pause, watch, pay attention. Don't make up your mind—just look.

I f you try versions of these exercises and you feel that you're ready for more, you can begin observing complex social contexts in different places or communities and try to find the larger patterns. This is what one of my students did when she decided to study the phenomenon of the "jam session."

THE EXPERIENCE OF A JAM SESSION

The student walked into B Flat, the underground Japanese jazz club in downtown Manhattan, long after midnight. On any other night, she would go down to the bowels of this mecca of music to hear the jazz she loved. Tonight, however, she was there to observe the background and foreground of the musicians. Against the context of the infinitely complex culture of jazz, could she discern the different ways the musicians were seeing each other and playing together in a jam session?

B Flat smells like an homage to cigarettes long ago stubbed out, and the lighting makes everyone look purple and bruised. Despite all that, this inconspicuous club is arguably the center of New York's music world. Adventurous and highly skilled musicians from all around the globe come here. It's not for the joy of playing or the love of music. That all happens here, but the student discovered that this was secondary to a more primary phenomenon: being seen.

Down the stairs came the musicians with their upright basses, guitars, cymbals, and brass. The student watched as each new musician checked the vibe in the room. Everything happened through gestures, style of play, and subtle expressions of musicianship and skill. The human brain can't process everything happening consciously—every move, stylistic choice, flex of skill in other players, and vast history of stylistic interpretation—yet the best musicians flow seamlessly through it. When the music is going well, they leave their heads entirely and just play with their bodies. Suddenly several hours have gone by.

Some musicians call this uncanny and highly complex skill "ear." Ear isn't just about hearing chord progressions and voicings but about reading the entire setting, the room, and the other players at once. Just like Gil Ash's experience, the background slows down for players with "ear." Their glaze of attention on everything and nothing allows them to hear a cell phone in the audience in slow motion. It gives time for one of the players to echo that sound with his trumpet and toss the joke back to the others. And then, as if time is standing still, the trumpet joke gets picked up by the bass and the piano and they both iterate on it, adding flourishes from other jazz jam sessions that also incorporated mobile phone rings. The group of players then take this mélange of patterns and sounds and toss it all back to one another as a repeating joke—both beautiful and absurd.

How long did all that improvisation take? Either less than a second or the entire history of jazz music. Both and neither. This is the wonder of the human glaze of attention. The intricacy and complexity of what is going on in this background creates the entire context upon which listeners like the student understand the night's music.

What draws people to a space like B Flat is this kind of interaction—it's more than just playing music together. After an in-depth observation, the student ultimately concluded that it was about the hope and fear of being seen by the right people in the right light. A great jam session is about bringing the right reference from a past jam session to just the right moment in the here and now. And pulling it all off with technical skill and panache. What the student observed is a "scene," a world of shared background practices. An astute assessment of jazz's hurly-burly at B Flat takes any musician far, but only if they also have the chops to get in there and play.

This phenomenon of *being seen*—a desire to stand out against the backdrop of the shared background—is common in many social worlds. It is different from trying to get people to notice you with outlandish acts or receiving unwanted attention like catcalling. *Being seen* means moving confidently through a shared world and making contributions that enhance or innovate upon that world. *Being seen* is receiving human attention at its most sophisticated and engaged. It is a feeling of deep belonging and respect from your peers, mentors, and the audience. Everyone, no matter what the scene, wants to *be seen* in some way. This is because all humans exist in shared social worlds. Those of us who experience a sense of exile or disconnect from our community—the mentally ill, unhoused, or otherwise disenfranchised—are desperate for this visibility. They long to be seen—to receive this highest form of human attention.

Take another example of being seen. This one's from the surfing community that William Finnegan so eloquently describes in his Pulitzer Prize–winning memoir, *Barbarian Days*. Surfing is far from a team sport and Finnegan is the first to say that "you could do it with friends, but when the waves got big, or you got into trouble, there never seemed to be anyone around."

Despite this isolation, surfing is essentially a social world—a way of *being seen* against a shared set of background practices. This is where style comes in. Finnegan's friend tries to claim that surfing is a religious practice, but he doesn't buy it. There is no deity, only the performance of surfing itself.

> Style was everything in surfing—how graceful your moves, how quick your reactions, how clever your solutions to the puzzles presented, how deeply carved and cleanly linked your turns, even what you did with your hands. Great surfers could make you gasp with the beauty of what they did. They could make the hardest moves look easy. Casual power, the proverbial grace under pressure, these were our beau ideals.

Surfers, musicians, actors, presenters, radio hosts—all these and many other vocations and careers involve the intensity of the stage. Your colleagues are not just judging your technical proficiency; they are judging your style. When you go out to observe people in communities all over the globe, you will find particulars and universals. Each local culture has its own complexities and peculiarities, of course, but often there will be universals across communities. "Being seen" and "seeking prestige" are observable phenomena that occur across all cultures and societies.

Another observable phenomenon across cultures is our relationship to death. One of my student teams observed social practices around dead bodies in New York and California. By visiting Hart Island in the Bronx, New York City's only potter's field, or "paupers' grave," as well as funeral homes across Los Angeles, they discovered that there was a front door and a back door to the practices of the world. The front involved rituals of mourning—some elaborate, like funeral homes' dark mahogany coffins and makeup sessions with a specific color palette for corpses, while the back door involved large-scale refrigeration machinery, logistics management software, and transportation for moving bodies from place to place. Their direct observation opened up portals to several shared worlds all at the same time. Our most astute observations often result from seeing fissure points between two worlds—a clash between the reverent memorial service upstairs at the funeral home, for example, and a refrigeration system for the corpses down in the basement.

Some of my students learn the most when they struggle with how to even begin. Avinash, an American raised in a South Indian family, enrolled in my course because he was taking time off from work to pursue an MFA in fiction at the New School. When I sent him out into the city to spend a month observing a phenomenon, Avinash's first experiences were disorienting. As a highly skilled engineer with more than a decade of experience in the tech industry, he habitually observed his interactions through a framework of utility: What is the intention of this process or tool, and how is the intention put to use? Although this training was necessary to be an engineer, it got in the way of his ability to pursue direct observation. Avinash had to set the engineering approach aside to pause and look.

He chose to observe an installation commemorating the extinction of the northern white rhino species at an iconic intersection in

New York. The sculpture featured three rhinos standing atop one another like acrobats. As of 2018, when the sculpture was erected, there were only three white rhinos left in the world. Because of poachers, the species will be entirely extinct when the last three rhinos die. Avinash wanted to describe the experience people were having while visiting this installation. But what was that experience? And why were they having it?

As Avinash stood before the sculpture in Astor Place, he felt confused, he told me later. What should he pay attention to? He noted the tourists taking selfies with the rhino sculptures. At the site people were soliciting funds for World Wildlife Fund and other conservation groups, using their phones and tablets to record donations. Was that important? He tried to follow the social media feeds and hashtags of the visitors, and he took notes on what they posted after visiting the installation.

All of these parts, however, didn't lead to a meaningful whole. Avinash felt himself flailing. As he made more and more visits to the site to observe, he began to feel that he was wasting his time. He decided to use his skills as a fiction writer to escape the discomfort he was feeling. Without talking to anyone at the site, he sat on a bench and began to write a story about the loss of the rhinos. When I read it, I let him know it was a good story and a bad work of phenomenology. He lost himself in an abstract idea that had nothing to do with what was happening in front of him. I told him: Get outside your head and look around. Strip away the abstract conceits and categories of thought that keep you from engaging directly with the world. "To the thing itself."

Avinash tried again, but this time he didn't approach the installation with a story idea. He didn't look at the materials and conceive of them as resources to be exploited. He took his inspiration from Merleau-Ponty and tried to observe the site from his own body. How was he standing in relation to the sculpture? How was everyone else standing? Suddenly, before his eyes, a social structure started to emerge. He began to see that there was a sophisticated choreography in the movements of bodies all around him when he stayed still long enough to observe it. The World Wildlife Fund volunteers were approaching people in different ways, and, based on the physicality of their approach, some were more successful at soliciting donations than others. The more Avinash observed, the more he could discern the pattern. The most aggressive volunteers approached New Yorkers by stepping right into their sphere of personal space. This inevitably resulted in the busy person moving away with a wave or a nod but nothing beyond that. Again and again, when the person asking for money stepped forward, the person approached stepped back.

The next group of WWF volunteers stayed at the edge of their own personal space and used smiles and friendly gestures to engage people and speak to them. Their charm made many people stop for a moment, but almost all of them quickly moved on without giving any money.

Then Avinash noted something remarkable. The volunteers who remained in conversation with people for many minutes—the ones who seemed to be getting not just the attention of people but their actual dollars—stepped backward at the beginning of the conversation. By taking one step back, they invited the people they were talking with to step forward. This little two-step dance imbued the exchange with the tenor of reciprocity. The volunteers were not intruding in another's space and asking; instead, they were offering their knowledge and passion in exchange for a donation. It was a conversation rather than a pitch. When Avinash followed up with more observation, all indicators for success—time spent discussing, relevance for both parties, and ultimately more money donated to WWF—were evident.

After observing what worked and what didn't work, Avinash talked to the volunteers. It was clear that they hadn't thought about their technique or which approaches were the most successful. But when he shared what he had observed, the volunteers started experimenting with his insights. More and more of them tried the two-step dance, and to their delight, more and more money was raised in the name of the last white rhinos.

When he began, Avinash didn't know what he was looking for, and he desperately longed to begin with an idea. But when you start with a model, hypothesis, ideas, or assumptions, you will often take shortcuts to decide to see that very thing. On the other hand, when you start with "the thing itself," when you approach the process with direct observation, you are scrubbing away all convention and conceit from your perceptions. And in the stillness of that clean break, you may well be looking at something that has never been seen before.

ESSAYS AND THOUGHTS

· ·

EXERCISES TO INSPIRE
YOUR PRACTICE

AN INNOVATION IN SEEING

USING THE LENS OF DOUBT

n the 1660s, a Dutch scientist and milliner named Antonie van Leeuwenhoek took a magnifying glass—a common tool at the time to look closely at fabric—and wondered what it might be like to use it to see other objects at greater magnitude. He started playing with placing two lenses together—one at either end of a long tube—to magnify the curiosities he put at the bottom. He constructed this homemade microscope and took it outside to see drops of rain. To his astonishment, he found in the droplets little creatures that appeared to be alive, moving around under the glass in a world that was heretofore completely invisible to him. This discovery of what he called "animalcules" alive in rainwater exploded his conception of reality and drove him to see more from other everyday aspects of the world. What, for example, would he see if he put his optical tube up to his own teeth? Again, he found what appeared to be an entire civilization of animals alive in his own mouth. "There are more animals living in the scum on the teeth in a man's mouth than there are men in a whole kingdom," he wrote in his notebook in 1683.

Today, of course, we recognize that Leeuwenhoek was one of the first humans to record sightings of protozoans, or single-celled organisms, an occurrence made possible only through the optical innovation of microscopy. This change in perception allowed us to recognize the presence of the invisible but potent microbiology that is a part of all of us all the time. With the invention of the microscope, humans were forced to concede that a world far smaller and yet far grander was omnipresent and pervasive. What's more, it had creative knack for survival that far exceeded that of any human ingenuity.

Just as the invention of the microscope allowed scientists to magnify vision and see reality as it existed on a smaller scale, other innovations in optics and lens making led to great discoveries in telescopy as scientists sought to see beyond the human world to the universe above. In the courtyard of a three-story terraced house in Bath, England, in 1781, an autodidact with an affinity for astronomy stood outside observing the night sky with a telescope he had created from a homemade metal speculum mirror measuring six inches in diameter. With his innovative new telescope, the young astronomer William Herschel meticulously observed the night sky month after month, season after season. On March 13 of that year, Herschel saw something through the lens of his telescope—the most powerful instrument in the Western world at that time—that he couldn't immediately identify. He described it as a "comet," but further observation of the phenomenon over the course of many nights resulted in contradictory notes in his observation journal. The "comet" had no beard and no tail. He was careful not to announce his discovery for many days, and his journals remark only upon his constant calculations and cautious observations. On March 22, he reached out to a colleague in the world of astronomy and described his finding. As more and more British astronomers weighed in, hindered by telescopes far less powerful than Herschel's, the scientific community reached a consensus. William Herschel had seen what no one else had witnessed since Ptolemy: a new planet, one that was eventually named Uranus after the ancient Greek deity of the sky.

Herschel's discovery—and the many observations that led up to it—changed much more than just society's understanding of the number of planets. With his meticulous scientific process, the world began to conceive of a universe much grander, and more immense than was previously thought possible. Whereas once the concepts of infinity were reserved for religious contemplation and mathematical conjecture, now scientists of the physical world opened their minds to its possibilities. Herschel's telescope showed us that instead of existing in a tight-knit universe where stars and planets were quite close but also quite small, we are, in fact, part of an immense universe that is anything but tight-knit. In fact, there is no known end to the universe, and it is constantly changing. In the blink of an eye, the scale of human life was suddenly exposed as almost insignificant next to this newly visible "Big Universe."

Optical breakthroughs have shown us that we are both bigger and smaller than we imagined—bit players on a stage set for the grandest of timescales. What we see and how we see it changes our very understanding of humanity's role in our world. This is why there is another breakthrough in perception that ranks alongside science's most important moments in optics. It is the story of a technical disruption that radically expanded our perceptions of each other. The maverick leader at the helm of this innovation—a German physicist named

Franz Boas—developed a groundbreaking new approach that al-lowed all of us to see and to analyze *other cultures*. His disruption, one that changed humanity just as much as the sight of Uranus or the vi-sion of protozoans, was to dismiss the assumption of the superiority of Western values and, instead, to devise a way of truthfully listening to and looking at other people. This new lens of understanding was a radical development born from Boas's training in the scientific method. Although it is not often cited as an optical innovation, no breakthrough in the age of modern science has changed so much about the way we see cultures—our own and that of others. It formed the framework for the field of study we now call anthropology.

The intellectual inheritance of Franz Boas—and the coterie of rebellious social scientists he mentored—is now so fully integrated into our everyday lives that it's hard to even imagine the world as it once looked and felt to him when he began his research in the late nineteenth century. When he started out from Germany for Baffin Island in the Arctic Circle to study the migration patterns of the peo-ple there, he was an academically trained physicist. In the period when he launched his career and started to teach at Columbia University—the early twentieth century—conceptions of human development looked very different than they do today. Race was still conceived of as biological destiny, sexual and behavioral traits were considered fixed, immigrants to the United States were subjects of suspicion car-rying disease and deviance, and the mentally ill were "benevolently" lobotomized to put them, and the rest of society, out of the misery of their existence. The role of the scientist in all of this was to stand de-tached from the detritus of humanity and culture and to categorize how each one mapped onto a continuum of social evolution. The study of humanity was a matter of finding a group's place along a straight line starting in savagery, moving up toward barbarism, and, finally, only for those considered white enough and of enough European descent, the arrow's end in the most exalted state of humanity: European civilization.

This was the theoretical lens that early twentieth-century ethologists had in mind when they went out into the field to collect their data. It was this hypothesis that determined what was worthy of observation and the same hypothesis that told them how to draw a conclusion about what they had seen. Boas, at the beginning of his career, was steeped in this same ideology despite a growing sense, throughout his early years of fieldwork, that it conflicted with the direct observations he was making. If, for example, he collected a bow used by members of an Indigenous community like the Kwakiutl in the Pacific Northwest of Canada, Boas's contemporaries perceived it as an object that fit somewhere in the "barbaric" chapter of social evolution. This was where the evidence was cataloged, and this was how it was displayed in museums: visitors were even led from room to room through the linear march of human progress until finally ending with artifacts displaying the tools and technology of Western European "civilization."

Today we still see too many vestiges of these morally hollow ideas, some even in the field of anthropology itself, but we can also recognize how much has changed. Culture was once seen as absolute, preserved in amber, and people were studied and measured solely to determine how successful they were at replicating the mores and the manners of the person doing the observing. The scientist observer was only ever on one side of the glass, while the subject—the "people"—remained on the other.

Early in his work as a field researcher with the Inuit on Baffin

Island, however, as well as with the Kwakiutl in the Pacific Northwest, Boas experienced anything but a set of universal and static truths of "culture." Instead, he lived through a constant disorientation of perception during his immersion in another culture. When studying the phenomenon of "sound blindness," for example, which is the inability of listeners to perceive distinctions in certain words, he initially assumed that he would identify greater sound blindness in the "primitive peoples" he studied because they did not use set pronunciation or spelling with the written word. What he discovered, however, was that each of us "perceives the unknown sounds by the means of the sounds of his own language." In other words, sound blindness exists in all cultures and with all people because most of us tend to perceive and interpret new experiences through the lens that feels most familiar to us.

These types of observations forced Boas to reconsider the scientific community's assumptions that humans are expressions of unchanging biological types. Instead, as he leaned more and more into processing his empirical observations, he found a more accurate interpretation of his fieldwork. Humans, he observed, are endlessly adaptable and ever changing—in both their individual bodies and in the communities they create. With the certainty of the evidence in front of him, he became an advocate for a new, more accurate understanding of human cultures.

This discipline "will not become fruitful until we renounce the vain endeavor to construct a uniform systematic history of the evolution of culture," he wrote to his colleagues. Boas was ready to let go of grand overarching theories and stories of progress and evolution in human civilization. Instead, he set out to lead a discipline that demanded the anthropologist divest as much as possible from his or her own assumptions, listening not to the sounds of his own language but to the sounds of another.

Throughout the early twentieth century, Boas headed up the nascent and chronically underfunded anthropology department at Columbia University, where he taught the female undergraduates at Barnard College before crossing Broadway to teach the mostly male graduate students at Columbia. In all his classes, he dropped his students in at the deep end. Instead of loading them down with theoretical frameworks or ideologies, he sent them off to complete advanced and independent research projects. He maintained that, as his students, they had two main goals: to observe and to gather empirical observations. This, he told his students, was how to do real science. Go out and look around, dig into your observations, and then, only after spending significant time immersed in your fieldwork, begin to formulate an analysis.

By sending his students out to gather empirical observations first—without any assumption or predetermined idea of what they might see—Boas was forcing them to ask essential questions about the scientific method. How do we observe phenomena before we even know what we are looking at? What prejudices change the way we observe things? Is it right to start with a set of ideas rather than start from scratch and see where our work leads us? In which situations is it okay to start with a hypothesis and test it? In which situations is it better not to have any preconceptions at all? The disruption Boas was developing needed a form of reasoning appropriate for limitless boundaries and contexts. The only way of seeing culture, Boas argued, was to identify a way to observe a new context. The lens he landed on was called abductive reasoning, but it might have been called simply "doubt."

. .

n the late 1800s, American philosopher and logician Charles Sanders Peirce, a giant in the movement known as American pragma-
tism, gave a series of lectures. They made him famous because he
found a way to define the three kinds of reasoning we use to solve
problems. Most of us are familiar with the first two: deduction and
induction. Deduction is drawing inferences where the truth of their
premises ensures the truth of their conclusions: if this, then that. Induction, in turn, is a way to draw conclusions from a series of observations. Both deduction and induction are core to the natural or social
sciences. With the idea of abduction, however, Peirce introduced the
idea that there is a type of reasoning that is less structured, but at the
core of insight. It is not better or worse than induction or deduction,
but different. "The abductive suggestion comes to us like a flash but
it is not a flash available to all," he argued. "It is an act of insight,
although of extremely fallible insight. It is true that the different elements of the hypothesis were in our minds before; but it is the idea of
putting together what we had never before dreamed of putting together, which flashes the new suggestion before our contemplation."

Abduction, induction, and deduction are each appropriate for
different levels of certainty. Deduction assumes that we know with
some certainty that a general abstract law (like in math or physics) is
true. Induction has a working hypothesis of what might be true and
uses experiments to test that hypothesis. Abduction is much murkier.
When we are immersed in a topic or a data set long enough, flashes
of insight can seem to come out of nowhere. Charles Darwin's description of arriving at his new theory explaining variation in animals—
the idea of "natural selection"—happened in a flash while he was
traveling in Chile. When he saw the site of a volcano with its layers of

ecological and geological information, the observation gave him an organizing principle for all the data he had collected. Had it not been for his obsessive and organized collection of tortoises and beaks of birds for many years, this abductive insight never would have happened. But the process wasn't linear, like deductive or inductive reasoning. It was the "Eureka" type of experience, where all the data he had collected over many years suddenly made sense.

Peirce contended that only abductive reasoning would allow us to observe a context and arrive at a new idea about it. Deduction effectively evolved a hypothesis, but it was unable to incorporate truly new and challenging information. And inductive reason limited the observer to one set of beliefs—all well and good for certain types of problems with set "knowns" and "unknowns," but no longer useful for problems involving culture and behavior. Each of these three kinds of reasoning has an important role to play in understanding the world. It would be absurd to suggest that abductive reasoning is better or worse than inductive or deductive. They are all just different ways to reason scientifically. Abductive reasoning without the rigor of empirical testing and organized experiments would be reckless. The process of falsifying abductive insight is not only necessary but ultimately also enlightening. What Peirce offered, in essence, was simply a way to consider the existence of abductive reasoning and the fact that it was particularly well suited for contexts with a high degree of uncertainty.

While the previous few hundred years had been about the development of science and the belief that deduction could conquer anything, Peirce, in his "First Rule of Logic," written in 1898, questioned what we thought we knew. "Do not block the way of inquiry," he told his students. The process of this inquiry held a space for asking more questions and kept judgments at arm's length. We long to arrive in the gestalt of coherence—the snap of judgment—but doubt is necessary when directly observing other people. Peirce referred to this necessary doubt as an uneasy and dissatisfied state of mind. He argued that it is our discomfort with doubt—not a lack of access to knowledge—that leads us to hold fast to outdated, foolish, and, in many cases, morally bankrupt ideas. For better or for worse, abductive reasoning is *uncomfortable*. Boas experienced this when he immersed himself in the lives of the people on Baffin Island. What was he looking for? He had an insight that it was a new way of looking, but he wasn't yet ready to name it. First, he needed to experience the uncomfortable sensation of doubt—the queasy feeling that he was in over his head, that he wasn't quite seeing the whole picture.

He encouraged his students to go after this same disorientation—the befuddled state of being that precedes insights achieved with abductive reasoning. This gave his protégés permission to set aside assumptions and preconceptions and engage directly with their own data. One by one, his students started to overturn the misguided and dehumanizing tropes that were accepted as truths across the field's community.

Margaret Mead, one of Boas's first female students, used a recent innovation in the field called participatory ethnography—or full immersion into the lives and the community of a people—to ask questions about a group of humans previously considered irrelevant to the male scientists: women and girls. While conducting fieldwork in Samoa, Mead engaged in monthslong conversations with the young girls who sat outside her lodging, and discussed everything from sex and masturbation, to infidelity, freedom, and autonomy. In her letters to her friend, lover, and fellow anthropologist Ruth Benedict, she expressed a fear that she might, in fact, be a horrible researcher. In these immersive conversations, Mead said she very rarely had time to do the cataloging and notating of the rituals and ceremonies that her colleagues in the field assumed were the real stuff of culture. And yet, when her hundreds of notebooks were collected and she spent time with the data in front of her, powerful insights began to emerge.

One of the most compelling was that perhaps cataloging culture was not always the best way to understand it. The taboos, rules, and events that Mead assumed would drive the behavior of the girls all felt far looser and more nonchalant upon actual observation and immersion. The girls she was getting to know didn't seem beholden to strict and unbending ideas about who they could, should, or might be. Instead, her experience of the Samoan culture was more improvisatory and based on individual contexts. Culture, it turned out, was not just about collecting baskets and making kin networks to understand who was allowed to name a baby. Instead, culture happened in the interactions of everyday life and the spontaneous exchanges between people. Perhaps most important for Mead's career, the thesis of her iconic ethnography *Coming of Age in Samoa* was that the girls she studied did not seem to experience innate gender differences. It wasn't a theoretical construct to imagine a Samoan woman holding a position of power, speaking out at a meeting, or casting a deciding opinion on an important community issue. All these occurrences were happening in the everyday lives of the Samoan girls and the mothers Mead was studying. She used her conversations with the girls and women in the village to show that it is not biology that determines how gender is expressed, it's society.

Ruth Benedict, a fellow protégé of Boas, took her inspiration from anthropology's innovations in other directions. After World War II, she left her post at Columbia—where she succeeded Boas as head of the department—to work for the US Department of State. While she was in Washington, DC, she used her training in observation to conduct a modern ethnography of Japan intended to help Americans empathize with a people that, only months earlier, had been their mortal enemies. Her book *The Chrysanthemum and the Sword* became one of the world's bestselling works of ethnography, selling over 2,300,000 copies in Japan. In its pages, Benedict was able to help everyday Americans achieve a level of awareness about the cultural differences between the Pacific and European theaters of war. She wrote, "More than any other social scientist he [the anthropologist] has professionally used differences as an asset rather than a liability."

The doubt of abductive reasoning coupled with an embrace of human culture in all its forms became Benedict's rallying cry as she argued that the purpose of anthropology was to make the world safe for human difference. The empathy she helped to create through *The Chrysanthemum and the Sword*—her analysis of the role of shame, honor, and hierarchy in Japanese society—did create a pathway for a more peaceful postwar transition. The book also provided a cultural context to help everyday Americans understand General MacArthur's decision to allow the Japanese emperor to remain in place despite his nation's defeat. Although MacArthur's strategy was designed with a political and military calculus in mind—keeping the emperor in place allowed for a stable transition to a new society under American occupation—Benedict's work as an anthropologist gave Americans a way of understanding why it mattered. To be sure, it had its limitations as a work of direct observation. No anthropologist working today would conduct research the way Benedict was forced to do during the war—relying on her Japanese colleague to serve as her cultural interpreter. Despite its flaws, the book did just what Benedict hoped it would do: it made the world safer for human difference.

Today, most people see the field of anthropology as either tainted by ideologies of the twentieth century or just plain irrelevant to life in the twenty-first century. There are endless feuds about who is subjugating whom, who has a right to observe, and what kind of field-work is considered ethical, if any. These questions of power—while important—have come to dominate much of the dialogue in the discipline. This is a shame, because while some of Boas's findings and methods now feel outdated, his technical innovation still has a great deal to offer all of us engaged in an observational practice.

Despite the openness with which Boas and his protégés approached culture and human society, he never completely believed in cultural relativity—the intellectual conceit that has created his legacy. Few academics at Columbia University were more vociferous in their condemnation of movements like nationalism and fascism than Boas. Even as a scientist in encounters with cultures he abhorred, however, he felt a vocational commitment to look first. Always look first, collect the data, try to understand. And then, only then, does a scientist of culture arrive at any conclusions.

It was this innovation that changed the world we live in—and the very people we have become today. Boas showed us how to see and understand others but—most important—how to use the lens of doubt to better see ourselves.

HOW TO LISTEN

Paying Attention to Social Silence

The year was 1959, and a young French anthropologist named Pierre Bourdieu was visiting his home in the foothills of the Pyrenees while on leave from the military. He had been focusing his research on far-flung locations in Algeria, but he realized during this visit that his own childhood village was just as deserving of an anthropologist's eye. Although he had known the province of Béarn his entire life, he had never really *seen* it. Could he make the familiar feel strange and look at it with the eyes of an outsider?

An opportunity presented itself one day when he went out to visit one of his classmates from primary school who was then a low-ranking clerk in a neighboring town. His friend pulled out a photograph taken of their entire class when Bourdieu and he were children. There were dozens of sepia-toned faces of young boys all the same age and from the same small peasant community. The boys stood in lines wearing the same drab peasant shirts and slacks. The group looked remarkably homogeneous, yet Bourdieu's school friend cast his hand across the photo in dismissive scorn and pronounced half of these young boys "unmarriageable." The children he was referring to, now grown men, were all the oldest sons in their families. In the agricultural world of Béarn—one that at the time revered primogeniture, the tradition of passing land down through the firstborn son—the idea that eldest sons would be unmarriageable didn't make any sense. More striking was the cruelty with which his friend tossed off the remark. *Unmarriageable*. He might just as easily have said *worthless*.

But why would these young men set to inherit both land and the agricultural traditions of their fathers be deemed worthless? Wasn't their status as the eldest born exactly the opposite?

This mystery stayed with Bourdieu throughout the early days of his visit. He was certain the word *unmarriageable* was an important observation, but of what? And why? He might have asked his schoolmate for more answers, but these types of questions—explicit and direct— rarely reveal meaningful truths about the subterranean structures that guide our behaviors and habits. His schoolmate would likely have said, "Isn't it obvious? Just look at them."

Bourdieu did have a bit of perspective on the province of Béarn that his classmates did not share. Whereas his friends had all attended local schools, at a young age Bourdieu left for a boarding school in the nearby town of Pau. After high school, his talents as a student earned him a scholarship to study at one of the grandes écoles in Paris. By the time he was a young adult, Pierre Bourdieu was moving in a world made up of the wealthiest and most well-connected families of France. This vantage point gave him some understanding into the insularity of life in Béarn, but it still wasn't enough to help understand the word *unmarriageable*. He would simply have to be patient and observe. Look—but at what? And where?

The Christmas holiday fell during this time, and Bourdieu attended the village's Christmas ball held in the back of a bar. Young people from around the region gathered on the dance floor. There under the lights, for all the town to see, was the next generation. Young men from the local high schools and universities were there, some of them from the larger town of Pau, as well as factory workers and clerks in the local bureaucracies. They were partnered with young girls from around the area. They came in fashionable clothing with their hair in stylish coifs. Two by two, they paired off to dance the Charleston and the cha-cha. All together and in time, the young people showed off their playful skill with this new music. They were the future.

Pierre Bourdieu watched the dancers, captivated by the excitement and movement that emanated from the center of the room. These young dancers were the focal point of the night. But then his eye was drawn to the shadows at the edges of the bar. There, in the background, he could discern a darkened mass. It was a group of slightly older men, all closer to thirty, standing at the periphery. Just as the young dancers were the story of the ball, Bourdieu realized, these older men were also the story. Unlike the younger men who moved with confidence in the light, the shadows could not hide the awkwardness of these older farmers. Their bodies looked stiff; their big hands hung heavily out of their thick, dark suits. Their feet seemed stuck to the floor. While in the foreground the feet all tapped in time, in this background there was not even a shoulder swaying to the music. Instead, the men were inert like rocks in the road—an impediment to progress. These, Bourdieu realized, were the *unmarriageable*.

When it was close to midnight, it was finally time for the bachelors to move toward the bar. Now they could relax and take up more natural postures—holding drinks, leaning against tables, and sitting on stools, looking at each other eye to eye. Away from the swirl of movement on the dance floor, their wool suits no longer felt so inhibiting. The young people left in new pairings, while the bachelors stayed behind and broke out into singing the old-fashioned Béarn songs. They sang into the night and, when no one was left dancing on the floor, they flopped their old berets on their heads and headed back to their farms.

Bourdieu might well have assumed the revelry of the dancers on the floor was the most important observation. But he had enough training as an observer to remain in doubt. If everyone was looking at who was dancing with whom under the lights, wouldn't it be more revealing to ask: Who *wasn't* dancing? Who wasn't the center of attention? And perhaps the most interesting and perplexing question: Who wasn't marrying?

An understanding of the foreground—the dancers—would be possible only with a profound understanding of the background as well, the world of the motionless bachelors standing in the shadows. For generations, a peasant's social standing was not measured by material goods like jewels or fine clothing. They demonstrated their social worth to themselves and to their community by accumulating more land. This wealth creation could happen through bountiful harvests, of course, but it happened more often through inheritance from father to eldest son. Until very recently, all social order in such villages spun on an axis around this social practice of inheritance. When Bourdieu was growing up, a woman from a small village in the area aspired to marry a peasant family's eldest son, who would inherit the farm, its land, and perhaps a small dowry. In his observations of the Christmas ball—with its background of forlorn bachelors—Bourdieu identified an insight: a seismic shift in what he called "the market in symbolic goods." These bachelors were facing a "brutal devaluation" in their worth because their marriage prospects were inextricably tied up in farming, land, and old-fashioned matrimonial exchanges controlled by their families. Whereas the young people on the dance floor moved with the freedoms of modernity—pursuing jobs in towns and leaving behind life on a farm—these bachelor farmers were trapped by their inheritances to old ways. The land they owned and the skills they had for working it simply were not valuable anymore. A new world—of trade, of mechanized farming tools, and a general globalization of every aspect of the economy—had shifted the ground under their feet. His friend's description of this phenomenon—one of the greatest societal and economic shifts to occur across provincial France in the twentieth century—was "unmarriageable."

After that night, Bourdieu described hurling himself "into a kind of total description, a somewhat frenetic one, of a society" he knew "without truly knowing it." Everything was data in his quest to understand the phenomenon of "unmarriageable": photographs, maps, ground plans, statistics, games played, the age and make of cars, the age pyramid of the population. Eventually, he assembled a system for seeing his own world. This rigor allowed him to test his insights against analyses of other rural communities across Europe and other areas of the world. Looking at the background of the Christmas ball in Béarn gave him a direct portal into seeing the emergence of modern society. He went on to write and speak about this new society, and his insights about the "unmarriageable" ultimately made him one of France's most celebrated twentieth-century intellectuals.

· ·

Almost everyone stops observing the minute they see those shiny, young dancers at the Christmas ball. Most of us take in the foreground and then—snap—we stop looking. We land on a judgment, lose curiosity, and stop seeing the greater context.

Taking note of the dancers does matter, of course. But what matters much more is cultivating an awareness of the hidden social structures that are happening outside the light. The best observers know that leaving the Christmas ball without seeing the lonely bachelors in the shadows is to miss out on understanding the most profound forces shaping our reality. The ability to observe what is invisible in a social context—what Bourdieu referred to as "social silence"—isn't only useful for an anthropologist in mid-twentieth-century France. It's valuable for observing any context because it reveals what really matters in a society.

Take our culture's fixation with tracking consumer behavior as an example. With big data and the barrage of statistics inundating our minds every day, we hear a lot about what consumers are doing. We learn that we are buying more snacks, downloading more content from streaming services, and ordering more home office furniture. But what are we *not* doing? What are we *not* buying? We base so many of our macro- and micro-decisions on large data sets that record what happened, but how much attention do we put on what goes unrecorded? When you ask who was in attendance, do you also look at who was left out? When a person is speaking, do you also observe who is choosing not to speak? When everyone is talking about a new trend, what are they not talking about? These social silences show us what matters. We can never truly know what happens in a place or a context unless we also know what doesn't happen.

No one knows this better than Gillian Tett, a masterful observer and an editor at large at *Financial Times*—better known in the United States as *FT.* Gillian has been covering financial markets and global politics for decades, and she is widely recognized as a media expert, in part because she ushered *FT* through a rough period when media institutions *were* forced to reconsider twentieth-century business models in the face of digitization. *FT* is now owned by a Japanese holding company and, as a Brit, Gillian has been the conduit between its Anglo-Saxon roots and the culture of the new ownership.

Most journalists in the industry, however, revere Gillian as an observer for another reason. She was one of the only journalists covering the markets to understand the terrifying depths of the Great Financial Crisis—calling out her alarm years before Lehman Brothers collapsed in September of 2008. How was she able to see what so few others could? And how does she continue to get great scoops on one big story after another? What gives her the ability to observe the visible in what appears to be invisible?

The answers to these questions go back to Pierre Bourdieu and that Christmas ball. Gillian Tett received her observational training while pursuing a PhD in anthropology at the University of Cambridge. Long before she was analyzing and reporting on derivatives in the City of London and on Wall Street, she was deeply embedded in a village in Tajikistan in central Asia observing marriage rituals for her dissertation research. It was through this training that she learned how to listen to the noise—what people talked about and said—while analytically observing the silence, or the things left unsaid.

Gillian is one of the most curious people I have ever met: she never really knows what she is looking for when she goes out to observe the world for her reporting. She has a sparkling personality, but if you watch her working, you see that she is almost always looking, not talk-ing. "Absorbing, not emitting," as she calls it. She has the anthro-pologist's eye: always trying to connect the dots across disciplines.

I have gotten to know Gillian well, so I wanted to ask her about her experiences leading up to the financial crisis. She told me about her first exposure to the world of bankers trading complex financial derivatives back in 2005 at a conference in the South of France. Like Bourdieu entering the Christmas ball, she kept her eyes open to both the dancers and the nondancers. She noted what people said and talked about as they each stood up to present their PowerPoints to the room. She was also keenly aware of what they didn't say and what they didn't present. In the slides, for example, the financiers used acro-nyms to describe their innovations—collateralized debt obligations became CDOs, and credit default swaps turned into CDSs—and they measured the value of their products with Greek letters and algo-rithms. Yet none of these conversations coming from the stage ever addressed how real people in the world would use these products.

"What was missing from the presentations were the presence of human faces," she told me. During breaks at the conference, she described countless conversations she had that centered on the craft of securitization. These, she explained, were usually predicated on the idea that markets needed to become more efficient. Yet in the middle of this constant chatter about increasing "liquidity" and creating a capital that could flow like water, she never heard a single human story.

"Who is borrowing this money? Where are the humans?" she found herself asking. "How does this connect to real life?"

The world in the conference hall was filled with patterns of be-havior as complex and hidden as those in the Tajik village she studied for so long. The bankers had a fluency in the emerging language of acronyms that described the derivatives market. Even though the attendees at the conference had come from financial centers all over the world, this secret code bonded them. No one else in the world could master this language or even understand it, and their knowledge created a culture of elitism. The financiers felt as if they were in on something exclusive. When Gillian expressed her own confusion over how the terms were used and the metrics for measuring their value, the rituals of explanation only added to the aura of their insiders' club.

"All the attention was on how smart the hedge fund managers were and how they were transforming financial markets to be risk-free," she told me. "And never on the immense risk of people not being able to pay their loans."

Just as she had analyzed the way information was disseminated across family networks in the Tajik village, she observed how the dedicated message system attached to the Bloomberg Terminal fomented even more of a clubby culture. Quips could go back and forth quickly on this messaging system—including references to complex mathematics inaccessible to all but the most highly educated—without any outsider ever stopping to ask for an explanation or accountability.

"The problem was that financiers could see neither the *external* context of what they were doing [what cheap loans did to borrowers]," she explained, "nor the *internal* context of their world [how their clubbiness and peculiar incentive schemes fueled risks]."

There were dancers and nondancers in that convention hall in 2004, but Gillian also identified the social silences that were occurring in the industry of financial journalism itself. Her world of media was accustomed to focusing its attention on the equity markets. These were the stories deemed the most relevant for *FT* readers—including dramatic human stories about entrepreneurs and CEOs as well as facts and figures communicating straightforward concepts such as profit and loss. The problem, she identified, was that her own industry spent so much time focused on these equity markets that they were missing the stories happening in the background. She called upon the metaphor of an iceberg to describe how the world of journalism was observing the markets.

"The bigger piece—derivatives and credit—was largely submerged," she described to me. While most of her colleagues were chasing scoops by looking at the tip, she could cast her observational eye on the submerged world that few journalists were incentivized to notice: the capital markets.

In spring of 2005, when she took over her new beat as the head of the capital markets team for *FT*, it didn't take long for her insatiable curiosity to turn to alarm. Just as there were no human faces on the slides and presentations at the conference, her interviews with financiers in the capital markets were almost entirely focused on abstract math, acronym-fueled debates, and a general detachment from any real-world consequences of the craft of securitization.

The foundational myth at the core of this culture—what Gillian referred to as the creation myth—was the story of "liquidity." Financiers in the world of capital markets all followed the same ideology: More innovation would create more efficiency in the overall global finance system. With this increased liquidity, all the risks would be dispersed across the system.

"Securitization distributed credit risks so widely that if losses occurred, lots of investors would each take a tiny blow," she explained to me, "but no single investor would take a painful enough hit to suffer severe damage."

This was the prevailing ideology. As a trained anthropologist, however, Gillian understood that it was just that: a story. If it wasn't true, it would mean a huge portion of the global financial system was at risk. In addition to other warning signs, she could see that these innovative assets weren't even being traded—far from liquid in nature, they were essentially inert. The CDOs were so complex that it was hard to even understand how to value them. With so few trades to draw pricing from, accountants had no way to measure their worth. Instead of using direct market pricing—what is referred to as mark-to-market principles—accountants turned to the abstract models of ratings agencies to determine value.

She used her role at *FT* to sound an alarm. In 2007, she wrote several pieces describing the inscrutability of the entire system, with observations detailing her sense that something was wrong. Of course, the market was still strong at that point, and she was called out publicly as scaremongering. She laughed when she told me about a financier who complained about her use of the words *opaque* and *murky* to describe these new financial innovations.

"He was certain he had full transparency into the entire capital market just because he had access to the Bloomberg Terminal," she recalled. "But most of the world isn't sitting at a Bloomberg Terminal. No one was talking about that. Nor was anyone saying that this transparency was an illusion."

As an anthropologist, she knew all too well that unspoken codes of culture serve those in power. Bourdieu calls what isn't said—what is socially silent—"doxa."

"Good observers look for doxa," Gillian explained. "What isn't said and what is hidden in plain sight. It is a kind of chip in your brain or X-ray vision that you get when you look at the familiar as strange and try to imagine alternatives to the way we do things. It really is a superpower."

In the summer of 2007, the faceless humans who never appeared on any of the PowerPoints or in any of the Bloomberg Terminal chats started to default on their real-world mortgages. Financial authorities tried to connect the global financial system, but the contagion could not be contained. In the fall of 2008, what came to be known as the Great Financial Crisis sent markets across the world into turmoil. A dozen of the United States' most important financial institutions all teetered on the brink of failure over the course of a week, and banks all over the world needed to be bailed out to prevent bankruptcy. Ben Bernanke, the head of the Federal Reserve at the time, called it "the worst financial crisis in global history."

The observational skill of a master like Gillian requires training, practice, and the courage to be a contrarian when it matters. She described the approach she takes in all her work.

"My process is twofold," she explained. "First, I try to see the strange in the familiar. I see myself as an outsider that observes a complex system that I didn't grow up in and that isn't obvious to me. It is obvious to everyone else involved, so obvious that they don't even think about it. But as an outsider, you have the chance to see how odd the whole thing is. What is familiar to others is strange to me. Often the conversation—or the dancing—works the way it does because it suits the people in control. The way they classify things helps people in power and not others—usually the powerless."

In the second step, Gillian uses these facts to try to imagine how things could be different. She tries to hear what isn't said and why.

She imagines alternatives to what she is observing. It is through this process that she arrives at insights about what she is seeing. What would that conference in 2004 look like if it were structured to serve a different stakeholder or constituent or consumer? Imagine if it were designed to appeal to the people applying for mortgages. What if the real people applying for the mortgages had to come in and meet with the financiers to complete their applications? Or if financiers in the system were incentivized to make their work more available or more accessible?

Whether it is dancing at a Christmas ball or presenting Power-Points at an investment conference, the best observers are always asking these types of questions: What do rituals of culture mean, and who are they for? Gillian's work reminds all of us to enter the world with both curiosity and doubt. Embrace the role of an outsider and ask what makes the familiar strange and the strange familiar. Never be satisfied with what people say. All the best insights are occurring below the sounds of conversation, in the submerged iceberg that sits unseen to most of the world.

Stop talking and try listening. What will you hear in the silence?

LOOKING FOR
CULTURAL SHIFTS

How Change Happens

grew up on a Danish island in the Baltic Sea—far east enough to touch the Iron Curtain. During my childhood in the 1970s and early 1980s, the fishing industry collapsed in our community, and all around me, former fishermen, the fathers of my schoolmates, were out of work. Men sat idle at home and in bars, and families struggled to pay the bills; often the kids were beat up at home and they brought that same violence to our games on the playground. The other boys my age found distractions in soccer and beer, but I could barely kick a ball. Instead of humiliating myself on the field, I spent most of my time hiding at home and in the village library.

Almost everyone I grew up with was Marxist. My family considered itself Communist, as did many of the other families on our island. Every morning of my childhood, I dutifully ate my breakfast of muesli and buttered bread while staring sleepily at the ever-present hammer and sickle hanging over our refrigerator. As hard-left-leaning

Leninists, members of the Danish Communist Party, we took our political cues directly from the Soviet Union.

To a child, of course, growing up Communist made just as much sense as growing up in a Christian, Jewish, or Muslim faith. We had central texts (*Das Kapital* and *The Communist Manifesto*), a founding father (Karl Marx), high priests (the prominent European politicians on the Left), and keys to the kingdom of heaven (the coming revolution). The revered books written by our prophet outlined the belief system: labor revolution would turn our world upside down, and the afterlife would be a working-class nirvana. In our town's central square, my family sold the Communist newspapers—with few customers—and we occupied our time with fundraising, organizing, and networking for the revolution. I was so busy throwing myself into agricultural and school-building projects—in Namibia, Cuba, and any other country sympathetic to our views—I didn't have time to reflect on the views I was espousing. I was enraptured by fervor—furious about the class inequities in the world. For a teenager, Communism was a totalizing, energetic, and angry faith.

Not coincidentally, loyalty to the revolution also opened doors to all the best parties. The Left was radical and hip. Communism was cool. There were youth schools, and youth camps to attend in Denmark, Cuba, and the Soviet Union, training the pioneers and Komsomols— their Communist youth. The Danish Communist Party had its own newspaper, seats in the Folketing, the Danish parliament, and an unquestionable moral superiority. Being a "socialist" was soft. "Democratic socialists," or social democrats, were betrayers. We often expressed more hatred toward the social democrats who ran the country than toward conservatives and the right wing.

Of course, in Scandinavia at the time, none of this was atypical.

About a third of the population identified as some sort of socialist. And as hard as it is to imagine today, most of the people around me believed that all this energy was moving toward a revolution—one that was coming soon. The Soviet Union was held up as the best example of a fair and just society on which we could base the future. The tenor of this part of my childhood was shaped by one consistent ideology: The world was divided into two groups—the oppressors and the oppressed. Capitalism was the oppressive system that kept people with resources in a position to dominate everyone else. That meant that the poor today were the direct descendants of the peasants of the past. And, in our understanding of reality, anyone with power over others, such as the person running the local primary school or the supermarket, was in on the plot to suppress and rule over the subjugated. If you were not oppressed, you were the oppressor. The framework was simple, but our world was rich with the symbolic meaning of class struggles and silent aggressions happening all around us.

Until, slowly, it wasn't. As I was becoming a teenager, the Soviet Union started to crumble. The hard core of the party and the community—including my own stepdad—doubled down on the ideals of socialism and Communism. The stories of the Gulag and the Stalin regime were plots to bring down the revolution. When I was old enough to seek out other newspapers, to critically assess movies and books from other places, it seemed increasingly clear that the principles of the Enlightenment and open inquiry provided more opportunities for social mobility. The men and women on my tiny island were languishing—the fishing industry was all but dried up at this point. None of our grand theories and consistent ideology offered any solutions to their despair and ennui.

Around this time, I started at a new school, and for the first time

I met teenagers who believed in God. These new friends invited me to eat dinner with their families. I watched in confusion as my classmates held their hands together and bowed their heads to say grace. Entire families spoke in unison in praise of an entity I had never once considered. And yet, when I asked them about the presence of this "God," they looked at me in wonder and shook their heads. How could I not see it? they seemed to be saying. Wasn't it obvious that there was an invisible order to the world? The certainty in their eyes was off-putting. Where in the world was this God they kept speaking about?

The religiosity of my new friends was alienating, but there were plenty of topics to distract us—art, music, and books we all loved. I didn't dwell on their beliefs until, one day, I sat with my own Communist friends around our dinner table and recognized a similar certainty in our eyes. We were discussing the imminent revolution and our hopes for the day when labor would rule the land. Nausea overcame me. My family's belief system—what I had always considered our reality—was organized around entities and ideals that were just as theoretical as the God that existed in the homes of my religious friends.

My revolutionary fervor began to curdle, and the simplicity of Communist ideas became claustrophobic. One morning as I ate my breakfast, I glanced at the newspaper strewn across my kitchen table and read yet another headline announcing the imminent revolution. I turned the paper over. I no longer believed a word of it.

On November 9, 1989, I was traveling to Berlin with my ninth-grade class for a few days at the very moment the center cracked wide open. The Berlin Wall fell, and with it any semblance of a cohesive order to my existence. It wasn't just Marxist ideology that crumbled away; for me, it was ideology itself. The confidence of feeling so certain about the world and how it worked just wasn't attractive anymore. I developed a reaction to anyone who preferred to find truth through abstract models, received wisdom, or simplistic frameworks without taking time to look around first. Without observing the messy reality of the world around us, no one can claim to know anything of the truth.

Of course, Communism has fallen so far out of favor today that it's hard to even imagine how we sustained that faith. Ideology in other forms, however, continues to pervade in all political movements, professions, and community groups. The experiences of my childhood inoculated me from the fevers of certainty that exist today all around us—whether it is the belief in a completely free market, the religious devotion to organically grown produce, or the mythology around already achieving a generalized artificial intelligence. These kinds of ideologies bear a structural similarity to the abstract principles that guided my childhood.

Following the collapse of the Berlin Wall, I set out on a quest to understand how ideologies take hold and how perceptions shift across cultures. To me, there was no longer any logic to history, no simple way to explain anything. How could people change their minds from one view to another—from one radically different gestalt to another—without any awareness of it? How do perceptions coalesce and then dissolve across political landscapes and entire cultures? And most important for the skills of the observer, can we see these changes coming across the horizon—almost as we can feel signs of a storm approaching in the air?

I found answers to these questions using the tools of an Argentinian political theorist named Ernesto Laclau. Although he spent much of his academic career as a professor of political theory at the University of Essex in England, it was his earlier experience with social change that inspired the creation of his analytical frameworks. He devised a technique to map out the permutations of social change that move like electricity through a culture. As a visual thinker, Laclau gave me a way to diagram and see the values and beliefs that move in clusters across society.

In his writing, Laclau likes to use the example of an earthquake. There is an objective reality: the eruption of an earthquake. But what does it mean? The significance of this event differs in different contexts. An earthquake is an expression of plate tectonics in one culture and an expression of God's wrath in another. We can all agree that the event happened, but if we have any hope of understanding the meaning of it, we must trace the value and significance of this earthquake from within its context.

Ernesto Laclau referred to the changing meaning surrounding each word as "chains of equivalence." The boundaries between what we consider good and bad, healthy and unhealthy, legal and illegal are limits we assume to be well defined, stable, and universal. But this is not actually the case: society is constantly changing. What about a word like *freedom*? Such a word is an empty signifier until we can connect it in a chain of equivalence with other words. Is *freedom* connected with *small state, low tax,* and *individual self-reliance,* as we often experience in the United States? Or is *freedom* connected with *big state, high tax,* and *lower levels of inequality,* as I grew up experiencing in Scandinavia? Both versions of *freedom* are valid for the context in which they exist. Freedom itself, however, is meaningless until it sits in relationship with other concepts. When we directly observe others and they tell us that *freedom* is their highest value, we can use Laclau's tool to visualize what they mean. Are they saying that they long for the freedom of living in a society with a strong safety net? Or do they mean that they consider their own personal liberties to be their greatest priority?

Just as I developed a keen sensitivity to ideology growing up Communist during the fall of the Berlin Wall, Ernesto Laclau honed his attunement to social dynamism during his childhood in Argentina in the 1940s. He grew up in a country and a culture under the thrall of the charismatic but unpredictable leadership of Juan Perón. Perón's political innovation was a combination of empowering the working class with social welfare benefits along with a vociferously anti-Communist approach; he never questioned capitalism or suggested that Argentina should socialize the means of production. In Perón's new version of Argentina, "labor revolution" was radically severed from Marxist ideology.

Bearing witness to these changes gave Ernesto Laclau a unique sensitivity to the fragility of the institutions and ideals each culture holds dear. The stories of history are told and retold in a process of change he described as "drawing in water." No drawing made in water ever lasts, he came to assert. During Perón's rule, "revolution," "freedom," and "socialism" were all concepts that were written in water—constantly changing and up for debate.

Today, Laclau's tools can guide all of us in analyzing our direct observations of people and social communities. What words and concepts do people use to communicate, and how can those unlock greater insights into the social context that guides their behavior?

Consider some examples. Is it good or bad to surveil citizens to protect the greater society from violent criminal acts? Do we connect surveillance with safety and security, or do we connect it with an infringement of freedom and a dangerous overreach? Is a just society one that prioritizes the privacy and individual rights of its citizens or one that protects the greater good by punishing behavior it deems unsafe or inappropriate? The world you come from will have a perspective on these questions that feels fixed. And yet rearticulations of meaning will change tomorrow what most of us believe to be true today.

When I discovered Ernesto Laclau for the first time, I felt like a bomb went off in my head. I read the main chapters of his book in one very long sitting in my little student apartment in Copenhagen, and I was obsessed with his books for years afterward. The background of my childhood was based on the material necessity of the working class overturning capitalism. I had absorbed its theoretical certainty, and any challenge to the structural analysis was a kind of heresy. These were the tacit and explicit assumptions of my youth. But here, in the book I held in my hands on that cold day in Copenhagen, was someone suggesting that the structures defining the world we lived in were constantly evolving and open to suggestion. Structures like "capital," "labor," and "democracy" along with countless other words and concepts like "freedom," "wealth," "science," "privacy," "health," and "protection" were not only possible to analyze and see clearly but were also liquid in nature. I had never been encouraged—permitted really—to think about how the world worked with this new fluidity. The relief. Here was a text that completely undermined the claustrophobic worldview of my past.

After university, I became a correspondent in London for a paper based in Copenhagen. I took advantage of the situation by asking all my living heroes if I could interview them. I met many legendary sociologists and world-famous philosophers, but the interview I remember best was with Ernesto Laclau. Enticed by the prospect of having pages written about him and photographers showing up at his house, he accepted an interview request from a twentysomething no-body like me. He was married to the famous political philosopher Chantal Mouffe, with whom he wrote some of his most important books and papers.

I prepared for our interview for weeks so I could converse with both of them about their ideas without the mess of political quarrels or any left-wing antics. I wasn't interested in his opinions about how the world should change but rather in the mechanics of change itself. I wanted him to show me what happens when people suddenly shift perspective on the way they see the world. How and when does change happen? And is there a pattern for seeing change in the future?

London can be very brown and muted in the winter, and the train to Laclau's house in North London was particularly drab. In all the rows of seats in front of me, I saw only mud-colored hats and scarfs. Out the window, a dreary rain fell against the blur of public housing apartments whooshing by. Suddenly the car doors opened, and a woman entered the train with a dazzling, bright red scarf. Against the background of a London winter's blurry black-and-white film, this woman stepped onto the scene in full Technicolor. Of course it was Chantal Mouffe. What luck. The two of us stepped off the train at the same stop. She walked down the street, her bright red scarf and lip-stick the only signs of life on that gray morning in North London.

When we got to the house, Laclau opened the door, and Mouffe breezed in and then disappeared. I was left looking only at Laclau, whose diminutive form resembled the small, brown ceramic owls that decorated his office. Although I was dying to talk with him, I also longed for Chantal Mouffe and the brilliance of her charisma to brighten up the room. Laclau served me a big warm glass of whiskey at 11:00 a.m., assuming it would benefit me—a kind and much-needed gesture. Then he sat down with me and discussed the structure of change until the room grew dark.

Throughout that day, Laclau helped me to understand that everything we assume to be true about our world can and will change. One day, there is a wall running through Berlin and then the next, it falls. It is made of stone and brick, but its meaning is ultimately fluid like the water that runs through your hands. Laclau and Mouffe call this experience of seismic change *dislocation*. Their writing articulates tools for anticipating it in several different scenarios: (1) during intolerable levels of unemployment, (2) during inequality and discrimination, or (3) with a currency collapse or intolerable levels of taxation. In all these periods of dislocation, they argued, there could be good cause for a collaboration across political identities or the introduction of a new, more convincing idea.

The legacy of their philosophy is most often associated with political theory, but I offer it here to you as an observational tool for understanding how change happens in any context or culture. I use their tools in every one of my professional projects to gain greater insight into the way people make meaning of their worlds. For example, does the upper management speak of company members as "colleagues," "collaborators," or "employees"? What do those words mean to the people who hear them? I advised the head of a major financial services firm who insisted on calling his employees "teammates." His subordinates found this insulting. Discord was rampant across the entire company culture, and management had turned to litigation to solve their conflicts. We looked at how a word like *teammate* was clustered with other values and beliefs—"equality," "comraderies," and "loyalty"—that did not feel authentic to the employees. The word *teammate* instigated a crisis of distrust across the organization.

How do employees in an organization give meaning and significance to concepts such as "colleague," "efficiency," or "good management"? How do management and employees negotiate the definitions of key concepts? Who has what interests in the concept's various definitions across the organization or the culture? Once I have gathered my direct observations in any project or endeavor, I turn to Laclau and Mouffe's visualization tools. Change is inevitable; your job as an observer is to find out where and how it will occur. The answers to that question can often be surprising.

This is precisely what our ReD researchers discovered when we partnered with the engineering team behind America's most iconic vehicle–the Ford F-150—to better understand how its drivers found meaning in words like *outdoors, environment, conservation, nature,* and *climate change.* The F-150's engineers struggled to see a future where their loyal drivers traded in combustion-engine vehicles for an F-150 electric truck. Was there a space to connect electric vehicles with drivers in a new way? Could we identify where change was already occurring— not in the foreground but in the background of social practices and beliefs? I offer up Toby's story as just one example of how all of us were able to see possibility for that change.

Toby's mind wandered from the dark road to thoughts of his new seven-foot rod and reel and the feel of pulling in a prizewinning red drum from the waters of the Gulf of Mexico at the southern tip of Texas. He and his son set out from Houston at 2:00 a.m. with his father's boat hitched up to his F-150. It was now 4:00 a.m., and they had to get the boat unhitched at the dock, get his live well full of bait, and get everything ready to fish before the sun came up at 6:00 a.m.

Even at 4:00 a.m., the temperature was in the eighties with the humidity close against his skin when he walked out to his dock in the darkness. Once the temperatures on the shallow waters of the lower Laguna Madre—the hypersaline lagoon between the mainland of southern Texas and the Padre Islands—climbed into the high nineties, the fishing would be more challenging. The harsh noon sun cast the entire lagoon in a flat white light that often blinded even the best fishermen.

Toby, who had fished these same waters with his dad for decades, had been looking forward to this weekend with his own son, Matt, all summer. His father had recommended a few spots to try—he was the real expert—but both father and son knew that catching redfish was about far more than finding spots. With his truck parked and Matt ready with the bait, they motored out of the harbor and set out into the breaking dawn over the lagoon.

Toby showed Matt how to scan the steel-colored water for signs. Most of the lower Laguna Madre was only a few feet deep—with occasional mud holes closer to ten or twelve feet. His boat was designed to skim over water as shallow as two feet to get closer to some of the grass beds. His eye barely registered the coordinates on his GPS, however, because it was far more useful to watch the ripples of movements across the surface of the water. The darker browns under the water's surface indicated a school—perhaps redfish, perhaps speckled trout. Toby wanted his son to understand how to read these waters, to learn to know the meaning of the wind blowing a certain way, the salinity of the water at different levels, the seabed thriving or dying, the mating cycles either in maturity or in a period of dormancy. The red drum liked to cruise around at the edges of the bed, so a relaxed but discerning eye could see them under the water as a dark mass moving in different directions. Toby also liked to cast his eyes over to the grass. Sitting still under an orange sun at noon—too hot for even the seagulls—he could see the redfish in the holes they created in the seagrass beds. An absence of grass meant the presence of redfish deep below.

What Toby longed for—what his father had caught several years in a row—was a prizewinning tagged redfish in the Coastal Conservation Association's Star Tournament. Every year, the Coastal Conservation Association—CCA for short—released at least sixty tagged redfish into the waters of the Laguna Madre. Any fishermen able to catch one of the first five tagged fish took home an F-150 Texas Edition XLT Super Cab. The contest ran from Memorial Day weekend until Labor Day weekend and only two of the first five fish had been caught so far. If he could catch one of the remaining three, he would take off the tag, throw the fish back in the water after weighing it, and drive back home to Houston in his prizewinning vehicle.

Beyond the prize, he wanted his son to see the bounty of the lagoon—a land of plenty for those who cared enough to value and protect its resources. That's why he slapped the CCA's sticker on his truck every year. Conservation was a way of life to his family: it meant conserving the traditions passed down between father and son, conserving the waters of the lagoon and protecting its plentiful resources from overfishing, and treasuring this time and practice apart from computers, email, and stress. The water was closer to contemplation, Toby thought. "Fishing." He slapped Matt's back, "It's good for the body, the mind, and the soul."

In his yearly dues to the CCA and in his deep knowledge and respect for the waters of the Laguna Madre, Toby was every bit the conservationist. Yet if you asked Toby, his father, or anyone else in his family if they were environmentalists, they would have chased you off their boat.

"Go home, bros," he and his cousins liked to cry out when they saw the wealthy bankers and executives hire guides to take them out on the water. Toby had the utmost respect for the guides—many of them were his friends—but the idea of paying someone to do a father's work struck him as pathetic. Only an idiot would hire a stranger to teach him to fish. And only an idiot would use graphs and charts to monitor the water's ecosystem. If you really wanted to belong here, you needed to do the old-fashioned work of putting in your time on the water.

Did Toby cherish his time outdoors? Hell yeah. Was Toby an environmentalist? Hell no. But what was the difference? Between words like *outdoors, environment, conservation, nature,* and *climate change* there existed a cultural distance as vast as that between Juan Perón's "labor revolution" and "Communist." The F-150 was keeping the lights on in Detroit—by far Ford's bestselling vehicle and the most profitable truck brand in North America. If the engineers behind the truck planned to make any changes to it, they needed to be certain they understood what the truck's values and concepts meant to its drivers. They couldn't innovate unless the changes felt relevant to Toby, his dad, his cousins, and the millions of people across North America who relied on—and regularly bought—F-150s for their daily lives.

In 2016, the F-150 vehicle engineers approached our team for an in-depth observational study of F-150 owners in Texas, Colorado, and California. The idea was to get a better understanding of the F-150 experience. How were the trucks working for women, for example?

Did the trucks have enough power to do all the heavy lifting, dragging, and pulling that F-150 users needed? What could be improved?

Laclau and Mouffe's theories on analyzing cultural change would be an essential part of our observational work. How did the F-150 drivers relate to their "environment." And how did that differ from their goals of spending time in the "outdoors." Before our researchers even went out for their weeks-long immersion into the lives of truck drivers across the United States, one message kept getting repeated both implicitly and explicitly from everyone in Detroit: going electric is off the table.

Starting in the 1990s, climate change activists had been proclaiming that manufacturing and sales of electric vehicles were tipping into the mainstream. In 1996, General Motors released its first electric car, the EV1, to great fanfare. It was intended to be a vision of a future no longer tethered to fossil fuels. By 2003, however, less than ten years later, the model was canceled, the customers were unhappy, and a new documentary called *Who Killed the Electric Car?* suggested that the auto industry would never have the appetite for producing mainstream electric vehicles. In the years after the failure of the EV1, Chevrolet tried and then failed with its hybrid model, the Volt, and Nissan's EV Leaf landed with a thud in the marketplace. American drivers, auto industry insiders assumed, were too concerned about the limited driving range of the cars, the underdeveloped charging infrastructure (especially in rural areas), and the significant difference in price to accept electric cars.

These were the assumptions. But while the US auto industry stepped back from electric cars, Elon Musk stepped forward into the void with Tesla and, along with other startups, showed the world that fully electric vehicles might be more than just a fad for wealthy people in cities. By 2018, Tesla was selling more than 220,000 vehicles, and its closest competitor was not even an American or European automaker. It was a Chinese state-owned company called BAIC Group.

Detroit was alarmed. Industry experts could see that the market for electric was growing, but it wasn't clear whether electric cars would ever go beyond buyers who wanted small, fast, and expensive. Elon Musk's Tesla and the nimbler Silicon Valley startups had framed the entire value proposition of electric vehicles around climate change: it's time to burn less fossil fuel to stop heating the globe. The pitch was directed at drivers who lived in urban areas like New York City, San Francisco, and Los Angeles. These were people who tended to work in white-collar fields and were comfortable with graphs and Power-Points. Seeing the charts documenting the CO_2 emissions data or measurements of ocean acidification felt of a piece with the way they got their information—in scientific and quantified data points. The Tesla spoke to these drivers and answered their needs: either committed environmentalists ready for lifestyle changes, or the less committed looking for easy steps to take toward cooling down the planet. In 2016, with the start of my firm's observational project, the discourse seemed set: going electric meant caring for the planet; it was a consumer choice that prioritized the collective abstract good over local or individual needs.

What we discovered, however, after spending time with people like Toby and his family, was that F-150 drivers were also deeply invested in a healthy and thriving ecosystem. Their relationship to the word *environment*, however—or to use the tools of Laclau and Mouffe, their *chain of equivalence*—was different. For the F-150 drivers, *environ-*

ment was a term that seemed irrelevant to the concerns and duties of their everyday lives. *Environment* was synonymous with a word like *rainforest.* It was abstract and far away. They associated it with the practices of people like those "bros" who paid the guides money to learn how to fish. *Environment* seemed connected to the wealth and elitism from global cities, involving pursuits far from the concrete concerns of the land: investment banking, corporate governance, software engineers.

When we started our global multi-year study, keeping electric off the table made sense. After all, trying to sell loyal F-150 drivers on ideas about climate change based on graphs and charts felt pointless—the ultimate betrayal—as well as doomed to fail. When our researchers went out and spent several months immersed in the lives of F-150 drivers, however, the direct observations they brought back began to tell a different story. Over several years, including hundreds of hours of recorded interviews and thousands of pages of ethnographic notes, and journals created by our participants, we realized we had to set our own assumptions about truck drivers aside and step firmly into the doubt of abductive reasoning. When our team of observers spent time with people like Toby, men and women who used their F-150s as constant companions throughout life, the possibility for a shift in perception was salient. Change was coming from unexpected places. A firefighter in Colorado named Rory took a precious night off work to drive his wife out to the mountains and park the F-150 on a plateau to watch the sunset. In the bed of the truck, he pulled out a blanket and spread out a picnic to enjoy a night under the stars. A woman in Dallas named Sharon hopped into her F-150 to leave her cookie-cutter suburb and get lost on the back roads of Texas, screaming in freedom out the window, "Where am I?! I have no idea where I am!" A farmer in central Texas used his F-150 truck to survey his land and cart his farm supplies. One day soon, he will retire and find sustainable ways to raise cattle on his plot.

For these people and the rest of our respondents, we realized that an electric vehicle wasn't necessarily off the table. Detroit assumed it would be a betrayal, but it didn't have to be. Instead, an electric vehicle needed to prove itself valuable in the everyday practical world of the "outdoors," not the abstract think tank world of the "environment." It was about changing the framing of an electric F-150.

Unlike the combustion engine, the electric motor's current flows through the vehicle the minute it turns on, and drivers experience maximum torque, or power, instantly. That's meaningful if you want to pull your neighbor's boat, or haul a trailer across the state for work, or go to a football game with your family and charge everyone's phone at the tailgate. An electric truck could help make life better for all these people, and it would have nothing to do with the discourse around the "environment." Ford could sell an electric F-150 to its loyal drivers and frame it with the practical assets of engaging with the outdoors instead of around an environmentalist's concern over fossil fuels. It would be the first time a car company tried to sell an electric car completely around the value proposition of practicality. Laclau's tool revealed a cultural shift from electric for "climate change" to electric for "fit for use."

In April 2022, Ford released its first F-150 electric vehicle, the F-150 Lightning. The company dubbed it "an electric truck for the masses" because its price point was comparable to the gas version of the F-150s, even slightly cheaper with the $7,500 federal tax credit. Its battery life gives drivers between 230 and 300 miles of range, so rural drivers can use it to complete the long distances that are a part of low-density living. They can conduct the energy-intensive tasks like towing, hauling, and off-roading that are so important to truck driving while also offering a charging infrastructure for camping, working from the truck, and powering tools (the F-150 has enough electricity to power an entire house for two days). In June 2022, Ford announced that sales of its electric vehicles had increased 77 percent compared with 2021, and sales were up overall by more than 30 percent. This was due, in large part, to the demand for the new F-150 Lightning.

Laclau and Mouffe's discourse analysis tools helped all of us on the project to see possibilities for change. As observers, we intentionally did not engage in opinions about how different worlds should or could change. Instead, we looked at the mechanics of how observable change was happening in reality. How did the gestalt shift for a group of people? And, most important for the vehicle engineers on the F-150, when? Identifying this change occurring in the background of the lives of the F-150 drivers revealed an opportunity to speak to that current coursing through the culture. As Laclau's tools illustrate, change is often happening without anyone even being aware of its presence. It comes to us "like a thief in the night."

OBSERVING DETAILS

FINDING PORTALS TO INSIGHT

L et's say you were born and raised in New York City in the early
twentieth century. Imagine the street life, the theaters, the sub-
ways. Before you learn to say your own name, you learn to take
comfort in the ambient din of people talking, laughing, screaming.
Lives are lived all around you, impervious to your approval or disap-
proval. As a baby, you move from your stroller fluidly from one mass
of bodies to the next—barely enough room on the sidewalks for all of
them. Faces constantly come in and out of your focus. As you grow
older, you become accustomed to people spilling out of every nook and
cranny in every street, stoop, and storefront. An empty corner or subway car is an anomaly.

When you are raised in New York City and you continue to live
there as an adult, you are never more than a dozen footsteps away
from another body. You sit close enough to other people every day to
see their eyebrows, whether they washed behind their ears, and the

stubble emerging on their cheeks. You can barely say a word without someone overhearing you.

Now imagine growing up in the Hill Country of central Texas during this same period. The first European settlers dubbed it the "Land of Endless Horizons" because every time they felt certain they had found the top of the final hill, they would reach the peak and realize they had countless more to climb.

How do we create a bridge in our perception from this first experience—that of life in a dense, urban, and cosmopolitan city in the middle of the twentieth century—and the second experience: a plateau so empty and devoid of people that the movement of a cloud passing overhead creates a spectacle across the land? How does a human from one such world understand a human from this other vastly different world? What kind of observational skills help us find common cause with one another when our sense of home is so radically different? From what imaginative place of perception are portals between us constructed?

One way to answer these questions is to learn from the masters. How do they use imagination to transform the raw data of direct observation into meaningful perspectives? In this chapter, we'll look at how to use the details in observation to arrive at insights.

Robert Caro was born in 1935 in New York City and was raised there. After working as a reporter for *Newsday* following college at Princeton, he decided to turn his observational eye toward one of the most iconic figures in New York City's history: the urban planner Robert Moses. Caro knew that if he told the story of one of his city's most powerful men, he would really be investigating a story of the powerless. With his focus on the proverbial dancers, he could better understand who wasn't invited to the dance. *The Power Broker*, his first great achievement of biography, was published in 1974 and chosen by the Modern Library as one of the hundred greatest nonfiction books of the twentieth century.

Observing how the mechanics of power worked around Robert Moses made Robert Caro eager to take on another legendary life, this time in politics. He turned his sights on the life of Lyndon Baines Johnson, and a career in politics that spanned close to six decades. His interest, initially, was in better understanding the political genius of Johnson during his years in the Senate and his tenure in the White House. In the first of his five volumes exploring Johnson's life, *The Path to Power*, he did not initially plan to spend much time observing his childhood and where he grew up. The original goal was to get some interviews about Johnson's childhood "for texture" to add into the main narrative: his rise to power and political genius.

In his 2019 book, *Working*, where he describes his journey to get those quick textural details, however, Caro changed his mind. The consummate New Yorker, a newspaperman who described his life as surrounded by "lively conversation all the time," arrived in the Hill Country for the first time:

> Suddenly there was something in front of me that made me pull over to the side of the road and get out of the car and stand there looking down. Because what I was seeing was something I had never seen before: emptiness—a vast emptiness.

As Caro reflects on that moment, he writes, "I think I realized on my very first drive into the Hill Country—or should have realized—

that I was entering a world I really didn't understand and wasn't prepared for."

All of us have encountered this feeling. We find ourselves ill prepared or even ill suited for the task of imagination and empathy set before us.

And yet, like Caro, we need not give up. When Caro hit his observational impediment—an inability to gain insight or understanding of his subject—he didn't fly back to New York and try to get inside Johnson's world by staring out his own city window. Neither did he descend into theories and ideology about country folk of the past. At the time of his research, there was no available internet, but he certainly wouldn't have used it to do drive-by reporting of Johnson's hometown on Google Maps.

What he did was put his body—as Merleau-Ponty would call it, "his perceptual apparatus"—into the lived experience of Johnson and his family. Caro knew that Johnson's mother, Rebekah, was isolated and lonely out there in the Hill Country, while her husband was a state legislator far away in Austin. It was a "harsher kind of loneliness, a kind of loneliness hard to imagine—that I couldn't imagine, having grown up in New York City." Rebekah's unhappiness weighed on her son, and it created a mood of mournful heaviness in his home and in his heart.

Caro needed to know more about this heaviness. What does the body do and sense during such isolation? What sounds does one hear? What does the sky look like? What does one even see coming down the road when it is never another person?

"What I decided to do to get a taste, a tiny taste but still a taste, of such loneliness, was to spend a whole day alone in the hills, then spend the night there and wake up the next day and spend another with no one there but me."

He took a sleeping bag and set himself up to spend two days and a night entirely alone on a ranch out in the Hill Country. In the darkness and solitude, he paid attention to all the noises and sensations that occurred all around him. "You find out things that you could never realize unless you did something like that," he reflected. "How sounds in the night, small animals or rodents gnawing on tree branches or something, can be so frightening; how important small things become."

These days and the night of isolation—the first of its kind in his life—opened a portal of understanding for Caro, another world, another life. He was able to see through the eyes of others, feel through their bodies, and imagine an experience of the night that was far removed from his own associations of nighttime sounds and sensations in Manhattan. It activated his imagination such that he was able to conjure up the perspective of Johnson's mother. "No matter in what direction Rebekah looked," Caro wrote in *The Path to Power*, "not a light was visible. The gentle, dreamy, bookish woman would be alone, alone in the dark—sometimes, when clouds covered the moon, in pitch dark—alone in the dark when she went out on the porch to pump water, or out to the barn to feed the horses, alone with the rustlings in the trees and the sudden splashes in the river which could be a fish jumping, or a small animal drinking—or someone coming."

Lyndon Johnson was, by all accounts, a complicated man. When Caro took his sleeping bag and literally slept in the place where Johnson experienced his formative years, he gained access to an insight that opened understanding for him. He called these pieces of understanding "revelations."

"In trying to analyze and explain aspects of the character of the complicated man that was Lyndon Baines Johnson, you find a part of the explanation in the character of the harsh, lonely land in which he was raised."

The story of Lyndon Johnson, as Robert Caro describes it, is one of power and ambition. The more he inhabited the world of the Texas Hill Country in the early twentieth century—the lack of electricity, the desolation, the hunger, and, always, the emptiness—the more he needed to capture the counterpoint to Johnson's ambitious arrival. What was the world of politics in Washington, DC, that LBJ found when he arrived there in 1931 as a congressional aide?

If you have ever spent time observing Washington, DC, you can imagine describing the world through the details of the austere obelisk of the Washington Monument or the beckoning facade of the White House. It was true that all these structures—along with the smoky taverns and the din of dinner halls where the dealmaking was happening—called to Johnson and, in many ways, created him. But Caro tells us that he still felt as though he were missing something essential in these details of his early career. What animated the ambition of this gangly young man: wrists sticking out of his sleeves and ears pointing straight out from the sides of his head? Caro had plenty of raw data—interviews with almost everyone who had ever worked with Johnson during those early years in Washington—and every single interview contained details about his determination and ambition. But what was the gestalt of these descriptions? How does it snap into focus from a distillation of individual recollections into the shape and form of insight?

"There was something crucial that I wasn't adequately describing in my writing. I wasn't fully understanding what these people were telling me about the depth of Lyndon Johnson's determination, about the frantic urgency, the desperation, to get ahead, and to get ahead fast."

After hundreds of interviews and time spent every day poring over Johnson's papers at his presidential library in Austin, Caro interviewed a woman named Estelle Harbin, who knew Johnson when he first arrived in DC from the Hill Country as a congressional assistant. She told Caro that she would see Lyndon Johnson coming to work at the Capitol from his modest hotel down by Union train station. His route took him across the length of the Capitol Building, and every time Johnson approached the building, Harbin told Caro, he would start running.

This piece of information had a curious effect on Caro. He could feel that it carried a weight in it, a kind of literary quality. The force of its strangeness demanded his attention. At first Caro assumed that Johnson ran to work because he was cold in his first real winter up north. But according to Harbin's recollection, he started to run only after arriving at the Capitol.

Caro knew from experience not to force this insight into focus before it was fully formed. Instead, he set out to walk this same walk himself—the path that Johnson took from his hotel to the congressional offices of his first job. He walked it repeatedly without seeing anything that might excite a young Johnson—certainly nothing with any explanatory power regarding his remarkable ambition.

Then something occurred to me. Although I had taken this walk a lot of times, I had never done it at the same hour that Lyndon Johnson took it, which was very early in the morning, about 5:30 in the summers, about 6:30 in winter.

Just as a portal opened for Caro when he brought his sleeping bag to the darkness of the Hill Country, Caro's intuition to mirror Johnson's footsteps at the very hour of his morning run also proved revelatory.

> It was something I had never seen before because at 5:30 in the morning, the sun is just coming up over the horizon in the east. Its level rays are striking that eastern façade of the Capitol full force. It's lit up like a movie set.

In that moment, Caro realized what Johnson had seen. It wasn't just the marble, or the columns or friezes crammed with heroic figures. A camera could well capture each one of these details with perfect accuracy. Caro, instead, was able to see the gestalt of Johnson's imagination. By channeling the full power of his analytical empathy, he could understand what these details represented to the person: the blaze of light and glory and the vastness of gleaming marble. They told the story of a grand stage set wide open and waiting for the protagonist to begin the epic drama. How different it looked and felt from the isolation and mournful emptiness of the Hill Country. How rich with opportunity for him to approach and finally play a starring role. The stage setting showcasing his majestic rise was put in place just for him, and now he had to get to work to make the myth become a reality.

"Of course he was running," Caro commented. Only after seeing it through Johnson's eyes could he understand *why*.

As Caro's insights illustrate, there is a dynamic relationship between the parts—or the details—and the whole, the gestalt. When

Caro connects to the details of Johnson's life, he discovers a portal into that world, an insight into something essential about how Johnson moved through life. Just as we shift back and forth between the realities of our perception, Caro was able to travel back and forth from his life in New York through an imaginative portal to that world. Waking up in his sleeping bag alone in central Texas, he brought himself to a place of understanding about the gestalt of Johnson's childhood isolation. This became just as real for Caro as the sound of honking taxis and the smell of pretzels from his own life in New York City.

If we have any hope of gaining access to another reality or another person's world, we must first set aside the contours of our own. When we look out at the world, we perceive figures, shapes, and sizes, and then we fill in the missing or ambiguous visual information from our own maps. Merleau-Ponty argued that this is where reality exists. For Johnson, it existed in the lonely nights of his childhood just as much as it existed in his early morning runs along the Capitol. But until we are willing to take our sleeping bags and sleep outside in the cold, we will never "see" this reality. The worlds of others will remain shut doors unless we can discover keys to them.

The first time I experienced finding one of these keys was when I was still young and perusing books at my local library. I picked up a title with the name Aristotle on the spine. Who was this person? What was he about? When I wandered into his world unknowingly— sitting down and reading *Physics*—I gained an insight that has taken me decades to untangle. The insight came from his description of the phenomenon of objects falling to the ground. Aristotle noted that objects fall down because they need to go home; they want to be where they belong. I read his explanation, simple and to the point, again and again. It struck me as ridiculous but also intriguingly odd.

Then I began to feel a disorienting sensation akin to vertigo run through my body. Aristotle's world—ancient Greece—had no understanding of gravity. In his world, objects fell to the ground because they were homesick. I am no Aristotle scholar, but the minute I accepted this observation as true and relevant, I was transported into a deeply empathic understanding of his time and place. For me it was a portal into a world of daily life that was radically different from my own.

I have since encountered that vertigo of coalescing insight many, many times, and it always happens in a similar way. I stumble upon an idea or occurrence that seems odd, curious, or just too absurd to be taken seriously. But when I think about it a bit more, it becomes increasingly clear that the people I am observing really think this oddity is true and perfectly normal. Not only that, this truth permeates everything in their lives. The observation of what is strange to me gains a kind of symbolic weight or even literary quality: it feels as if it somehow fits into a bigger and more important story. Just as Aristotle's ideas about gravity opened up the world of Aristotelian physics that dominated Western culture until Isaac Newton, seemingly small observations can be a key to a much bigger understanding of internal logic. What *is* the belief that objects need to go home where they belong? When I read those words and began to understand what they meant, I experienced a gestalt shift from *gravity* to *objects experience homesickness*. Robert Caro shifted from *urban connectivity* to *rural isolation*. It is when we follow this trail of the odd or strange that we wind up with inquiry and insight: we start to ask questions we haven't asked before and to think about the world in ways we never expected.

In pursuing the curious and the uncanny, we pay less attention to *what* cultures and people are thinking and instead our focus is on *how* they think. What structures make up their experiences, and how do they navigate them? After my adolescent discovery with Aristotle, I found that this same observational practice could transform the seemingly mundane details of my life into rich, complicated structures. The bureaucrats pushing their papers around in Copenhagen's city offices became as fascinating and worthy of study as the fine art on display in the National Gallery of Denmark. The people dispatched to clean up after the pigeons in Piccadilly Circus had values and orientations as sophisticated as the dons crossing the cobblestone streets of Oxford University. Invisible worlds reveal themselves if you deem them worthy of your focus and attention. In this way, the average and the everyday become magical, and you learn that life is saturated with meaning.

In Wertheimer's Looking Lab, he referred to this as figure-ground: in order to perceive a figure, you must also perceive the ground behind it. This is why optical illusions are so often used to exemplify gestalt theories, because they call attention to the way our perception relies on the context of the foreground and the background. You never actually see something—you cannot achieve a meaningful observation—unless you are seeing it in its full context. When we extend these ideas to include our analytical empathy, it explains how Caro could "see" Johnson only when he understood the depth of his early isolation.

As Caro illustrates, one of the most extraordinary human abilities is our capacity to pay close attention to details in the lives of other people without losing our sense of their whole: We can analyze the figure without ever losing awareness of the ground. We can see a ring on a jeweler's counter, for example, and understand that the couple next to us are looking at it to celebrate their upcoming wedding. We can pay attention to details like the cut and color of the jewel, and these details serve to enrich our empathic understanding of the couple and their excitement for the romantic adventure that awaits them.

When you set out to observe, you are not seeking to put a spotlight on the details. You are cultivating attention that allows you to perceive the whole—the whole of the couple's romance, for example, or the whole of Johnson's path to power. You don't want to pay attention to just one detail or another. The power of an insight comes when our attention shifts with dexterity between the details and the entire phenomenal field.

Robert Caro shows us how to master observing these details and transforming them into insights. There is another writer—fiercely idiosyncratic and endlessly inventive in his ambitions—who offers us an example of what it looks like to fail. What happens when we observe raw data with fastidious attention to detail without ever acknowledging the background, or the ground, upon which that detail happens? What does it mean to see a place like Thirteenth Street—a fashion student, a school, a truck, or a car—without acknowledging the whole hurly-burly of all human actions? These are the very questions that animated one of the most spectacularly unsuccessful works of observation ever put down to paper.

Georges Perec was born in 1936 to a Jewish family from Poland in a working-class district of Paris. His childhood was filled with trauma—his father died as a young man serving as a soldier in World War II, and his mother was murdered in a Nazi concentration camp. Few of his works describe these devastating events in any autobiographical detail, but all his artistic experiments—which took the form of films, plays, essays, and novels—explore failure, absence, constraint, and a world order characterized by cosmic ambivalence. In 1965, one of his first works of fiction, *Les choses: Une histoire des années soixante* (translated in English as *The Things: A Story of the Sixties*) was published to great acclaim in France, earning him the Prix Renaudot literary prize. The book's protagonists—a young couple disengaged with their work as market researchers—spend all their time cataloguing the luxurious thing they buy, have bought, or long to buy in the future. The first chapter might well be a satirical take on a real estate ad with its pages of details describing a lavishly appointed apartment. The novel's opening line sees nothing of the characters—only a desirous "eye" taking in opportunities for acquisition: "L'œil, d'abord, glisserait sur la moquette grise d'un long corridor, haut et étroit [The eye, at first, would glide over the grey carpet of a long hallway, tall and narrow]."

When the book was published, it was immediately embraced by France's nonconformist youth culture. Angry over the war in Algeria and France's role as a colonist bully, they longed for Georges Perec to fit their mold of a political artist wielding a satirical sword of Marxist critique. He could be their mascot: the writer of a generation to critique a French culture caught in a capitalist fever dream.

Perec, however, refused. Instead of focusing on political or sociological critique, he moved in a direction far more idiosyncratic. Like all ambitious observers, he longed for a way to observe the world without ideology or closed systems of thoughts—what he referred to as "terrorist systems." Instead, in an article he published in 1973, he called for a new way of seeing the world. Enough with the news, reportage, and journalism as a whole, he argued. These modes of representing reality are interested only in observing the exotic and the unusual. Georges Perec wanted to describe not the extraordinary, but the most ordinary.

Where is the rest of it, the rest of our lives, the rest of what really happens? How can we give an account of what goes on every day and goes on going on from day to day—the banal, everyday, obvious, common, ordinary, infraordinary, habitual background noise of living? How do we approach it, how can we describe it?

Perec's manifesto was not so different from the work Boas conducted when he went to Baffin Island for his first study of migration. While he was alone and isolated from his own culture, he found out what was ordinary and everyday in the background practices of the Inuit people. This perspective gave him a new way of seeing the practices of his own culture as a German physicist educated and raised in the nineteenth century.

Perec wanted something even more radical than Boas and his first group of anthropologists, however. He urged his readers to completely forgo the study of other cultures that brought them far away from themselves and, instead, create a discipline focused only on what he called "the invisibilia" of ordinary life. This was a call for a new kind of observational practice, one "that will elicit from us what we have for so long stolen from others: not exotics but endotics."

What we must question is bricks, concrete, glass, our table manners, our utensils, our tools, our timetables, our rhythms of living. Question whatever seems to have ceased to surprise you forever. We are alive, to be sure; we breathe, no doubt about it; we walk, we open doors, we go downstairs, we sit at tables to eat, we lie down in a bed to sleep. How? Where? When? Why?

Describe the street you live in. Describe another. Compare.

As if in response to his own assignment, Georges Perec did just that. He brought his notebook and a pen and sat down at place Saint-Sulpice in Paris for three days in October 1974. He began his observation by detailing in a short paragraph what was usually seen and described in Saint-Sulpice, things like "a district council building, a financial building, a police station, three cafés, one of which sells tobacco and stamps, a movie theater, a church on which Le Vau, Gittard, Oppenord, Servandoni, and Chalgrin have all worked, and which is dedicated to a chaplain of Clotaire II, who was bishop of Bourges from 624 to 644 and whom we celebrate on 17 January."

This is a partial list of what most of us see on any ordinary day at that street corner. But what of the rest of the details? What happens when we try to observe what gets left out of the picture? What does it look like to see what is so ordinary and everyday that it does not even leave an impression across our awareness?

My intention in the pages that follow was to describe the rest instead: that which is generally not taken note of, that which is not noticed, that which has no importance: what happens when nothing happens other than the weather, people, cars, and clouds.

The point of such an exercise—what Perec referred to as "endotics," or the opposite of the exotics—was not dissimilar from the goals of other masters' observations. Perec wanted to do something both obvious and radical: to look without any preconceived notion. To see himself seeing. And so his "attempt" begins:

Outline of an inventory of some strictly visible things:

—Letters of the alphabet, word: "KLM" (on the breast pocket of someone walking by), an uppercase "P" which stands for "parking"; "Hotel Recamier," "St-Raphael," "l'epargne a la derive [Savings adrift]," Taxis tete de station [Taxi stand], "Rue du Vieux-Colombier," "Brasserie-bar La Fontaine Saint-Sulpice," "P ELF," "Parc Saint-Sulpice."

Georges Perec makes an attempt at describing Saint-Sulpice through what is utterly ordinary and invisible. What is missing, however, and what makes his work only an "attempt" and not an accomplishment, is the lack of a whole. Unlike Caro's description of Lyndon Johnson's morning run, there are only details here and no gestalt. We never once find the portal that takes us to this specific corner of Paris on this specific October day in 1974.

The 63 goes to Porte de la Muerte

The 86 goes to Saint-Germain-des-Pres

Cleaning is good, not making a mess is better

A German bus is better

A Brinks bus

The 87 goes to Champs-de-Mars

The 84 goes to Porte Champerret

He lists colors, "blue bag / green shoes / green raincoat / blue taxi / blue 2cv," but what do they mean? Why does it matter that one person chose to use that particular blue bag while another chose to wear green shoes? What kind of shoes and for what kind of event? Are they pinched and uncomfortable, or are they sensible and spacious? How does any of it appear to the people who live and work in this place

Saint-Sulpice? Most important, what does it mean to Georges Perec? There is no "unmarriageable" mystery animating his effort, no path to power to understand.

Because Georges Perec constrains himself from finding a portal of understanding to these questions, his piece remains not art, but an attempt. In its English publication, translator Marc Lowenthal even called it *An Attempt at Exhausting a Place in Paris.* Perec fails, and surely intentionally, because he is not revealing what this list of the ordinary and invisible means in its context. He details "a man with a pipe and black satchel." But this detail alone tells us nothing about the world of Saint-Sulpice. A pipe and a black satchel are connected to many worlds: that of the 1970s businessman on his way to work, of the pensioner wandering through town, of a fashionista playing with accessories. They have meaning to us, and that *meaning* is what we see first when we see a pipe and a satchel.

I can imagine Perec reading Merleau-Ponty and setting himself up in an imaginary artistic challenge with his philosophy. When he details "pipe" and "satchel," how long can we withhold a meaningful gestalt—or organized whole? Who is using these things? For what purpose? What background practices make up their behavior and why? In his attempt, Perec has given us all the details of the city street without any of the gestalt. What is the world?

Of course, Perec understands his limitations, and, by the end of his "attempt," he seeks out any details that will allow his observations to differentiate. By October 19, 1974, he shows us the weariness of detailing the obvious and ordinary.

What has changed here since yesterday? At first sight, it's really the same. Is the sky perhaps cloudier? It would really be subjective to say that there are, for example, fewer people or fewer cars. There are no birds to be seen. There is a dog on the plaza. Over the hotel Recamier (far behind it?) a crane stands out in the sky (it was there yesterday, and I don't recall making note of it). I couldn't say whether the people I'm seeing are the same ones as yesterday and whether the cars are the same ones as yesterday. On the other hand, if the birds (pigeons) came (and why wouldn't they come) I'd feel sure they would be the same birds.

Does his attempt ever take us to Saint-Sulpice? No. Georges Perec wrote his original manifesto with specific challenges to detail life as it is lived in its most invisible nooks and crannies:

> Make a list of the content of your pockets, of your handbag. Query the origin, the use, and the future of every one of the objects you find.
>
> Interrogate your teaspoons.
>
> What's under your wallpaper?
>
> How many movements do you have to make to dial a telephone number? Why?
>
> Why can you not buy cigarettes at the chemist's? Why not?
>
> It matters little to me that these questions are fragmentary, barely indicative of a method, at the most a pointer to a project. It matters a great deal that these questions should seem trivial and futile. That is precisely what makes them at least essential, if not more so, than so many other questions by means of which we have tried in vain to tune into our truth.

As you practice your skills, using the intellectual bravery of Georges Perec's manifesto but the fastidious compassion of Robert Caro's execution as your guide, you will start connecting your details with your overall gestalt. In learning how to observe and describe details, we begin training ourselves to see the foreground as it relates to the background, to cultivate these skills of hyper-reflection. We work to hold ourselves still to see how different worlds make meaning.

If you are unable or unwilling to spend the night on the dusty expanse of the Texas Hill Country, your observations will not contain anything with explanatory power. Therefore, you must train. Bring yourself to the practice: observations without a "you" somewhere inside of them are just lists. Obsessively and intentionally follow your data. Pay attention to what is funny, strange, or odd. Sacrifice your own comfort so you can go out and take a look around.

SEEING THE FUTURE
IN THE PRESENT

The Story of My Looking Lab

For Donald Judd, James Turrell, and Seth Cameron, it was the body in light, color, and space. For Ernesto Laclau and Chantal Mouffe, it was societal change. For Robert Caro, it was Lyndon Johnson's power and ambition. For Maurice Merleau-Ponty, it was the phenomenology of perception itself.

For me, well, it was the remote control.

Why on earth, I wondered in the early 2000s, would anyone still be using a remote control to watch television and paying money for a package of synchronous programming? Why did they sit inert in front of a rectangle of bad design and resign themselves to stories and ideas on someone else's schedule? It seemed so odd to me that people would drone through hundreds of channels only to start all over when they had circled through them all. The strangeness of the remote control and the hundred-dollar cable subscription was a portal into the future of media. I was compelled with an obsessive desire to find out: *Why would humans behave that way?*

Simon Critchley, my friend and collaborator on the Human Observation course, argues that all philosophy comes from a deep sense of disappointment about the world. Merleau-Ponty felt disappointed with the way the tradition of hundreds of years of philosophy—beginning with Descartes—had described our experience of perception. He simply had to create something better, something more accurate. It wasn't a choice; it was an imperative. Disappointment drove his philosophy forward on a path toward a new and better articulation of our experience of being human.

I would also argue that the same force is driving all creative endeavors. In our disappointment with the practices that make up our daily lives—social media that drives us further apart, technology that doesn't work, health care that makes us sick—creative thinkers follow their disappointment to come up with better insights and ultimately better solutions.

It was this sense of disappointment that characterized my obsession with the remote control. As small and inconsequential as it sounds, I saw its limitations everywhere. I would hear people complaining about their cable subscription packages or the frustrations of nothing to watch after work. I'd pick up remote controls in hotels all across the world and in my every encounter with them, my disappointment would grow: *Why is this so unsatisfying—stupid, really?* Of course, other obsessions were compelling me at the time as well. Pockets of human behavior that didn't make any sense to me. The practice of yoga moving away from the sphere of spirituality and into the world of sport. The technology of driverless cars misunderstanding human perception. Connectivity creating more chasms rather than bridges in communities all over the world. People refusing to take the medicine that would make their lives better and longer. These were the questions I was constantly trying to answer, the direct observations I kept trying to make.

You don't need a reason beyond your own obsessive curiosity to follow a phenomenon—your practice doesn't have to make the world a better place, disrupt an entire industry, or add to the academic literature on one finding or another. In fact, if you are beginning your inquiry with any of these goals, you will likely fall far short. What you need to begin is a drive to understand the human behavior and the social world that perplexes you. Why on earth would people do such things?

In my early twenties, I thought academia was the place where I could follow any phenomenon I felt driven to explore. Academia, after all, is sold to students as an arcadia of freedom and intellectual inspiration. The reality, as I found it, was much different. The academics I spent time with didn't seem to be having much fun. A few were, but it wasn't the norm. Even more grim, their "fun" was seen as suspicious. The professors working at universities spent much of their time fighting over unreasonably limited resources while academic bureaucracies grew more bloated. It just wasn't for me.

After that, I thought journalism would be a place for me to roam widely. I worked for a small independent newspaper in both Denmark and London and enjoyed it thoroughly, but I couldn't help but see that something was wrong with the media world. In the early 2000s, the decline in advertising and the move toward real-time news online was taking its toll on print-based media. My colleagues hated the changes that were undermining their livelihoods and work practices. Every editorial meeting was an early microcosm of the industry's twentieth-century swan song. The mood in newsrooms was dour, and I felt as if the coming decades would be only more miserable with people getting laid off every six months. By the time I left journalism, most of the budgets for investigative journalism had evaporated. It was time to move on. But where?

The curiosity driving my questions grew in scale, and I knew the insights I was seeking were global, not local. If I really wanted to find answers to questions about, say, the future of cooking, how people relate to their money and banking, the role of winning and losing in artificial intelligence, and how perception works in autonomous vehicles, I was going to need to scale. The projects I envisioned required a group of highly skilled fellow observers around me to help gather and process data. I would need them to be different from me, from different places with different cultural backgrounds to keep my own assumptions and intellectual laziness in check. If the people you work with look and think like you, something is wrong.

I would also need significant resources to sustain the research until we arrived at insights. This meant significant research budgets to send observers all over the world to collect data and plenty of time to sustain an in-depth observational process. Given all this, there seemed to be only one path forward for my professional and vocational life. I was going to have to start my own Looking Lab.

And yet you can't start a company on your own. Or at least, I didn't want to. During this period, I was fortunate to share many of my obsessions with respected colleagues and friends. Filip Lau lived six hundred feet away from the house I grew up in, and the two us attended high school together. After going on to study sociology and philosophy respectively at university, he and I would often come together to share thoughts about the curiosities that were driving our research. More and more, we felt aligned in our interest to bring methodologies and observational practices from our academic fields of sociology and philosophy into a bigger world. I met Mikkel B. Rasmussen around this time—he was working as a civil servant in the Danish government—and the two of us quickly found common cause both with our disappointments in our respective siloed bureaucracies and with our goals for the future. I still haven't met a more creative person or someone who inspires me more. Filip, Mikkel, and I decided to build a company together to follow our shared interests. Later we met Charlotte Vangsgaard and Jun Lee, not present at the company's founding but as close to being founders as you can get.

If all of us were French and lived in the middle of the twentieth century, we might have found a hospitable home in academia. If we had met in the 1970s, we probably would have founded a print magazine, a band, or a record label. As it happened, we met in the early 2000s, and the organization that felt the most exciting—offering the most freedom accompanied by the biggest budgets to pursue our every freewheeling intellectual interest—was a consultancy. To call it a consultancy, however, is misleading. Most consultancies are structured around meeting the clients' needs. Our goal was never anything other than sating our own curiosity. Clients might come to us with a specific issue, but we always found a way to turn it into a phenomenon we were genuinely interested in exploring. This left us in a unique position to turn down work that didn't help us address one of our deeper intellectual obsessions. The resources required to do our work well also eventually ruled out any companies too small or departments too far removed from the executive suite. When you want to do research on the biggest questions, it turns out the only people in a position to make any use of it are also the people in charge. That suited us fine—as long as we received the resources to do our large-scale research with both integrity and rigor, we would happily share our findings and ideas with the C-suite.

On a whim, we ended up calling ourselves ReD Associates. The name didn't mean much, but that irreverence was important too: we never wanted our group to become a symbol of ideology or a "five-point" secret to success. Our worst nightmare was a PowerPoint deck proclaiming our branded methodology. Our shared sensibility was a deep skepticism of any dogma or ideological framework clouding the potency of clean, direct observation. Our offering to the market in all this was the only attribute that ever delivers insights: follow the phenomenon and see where it takes you.

As a result, we created a company that was completely idiosyncratic and, in many ways, completely self-indulgent. We didn't mind that what we did helped the corporations or institutions that hired us. But we did it for ourselves. The insights and ideas we discovered were the ultimate reward. Conveniently enough, they also broke open creative opportunities and solutions for our clients in strategy, product development, and innovation, and made billions for their companies.

Over the years, ReD has hired more than a thousand people to help in our efforts, and we have spent hundreds of millions of dollars on research to carry out our work. We hired the most intelligent, diverse, and skilled observers from across the globe—luring them away from academia with the promise of scale, more freedom, more fun—and we sent them all over the world to study countless questions of culture and behavior that perplexed us. Together, along with new partners and the hundreds of associates who joined us for the ride over the years, we opened offices in Copenhagen, New York City, London, Paris, Hamburg, and Shanghai. We created a setup where we could commit enormous resources to serve whatever whim of interest we had in pretty much anything. We knew that most of the time we could make that helpful for companies or other kinds of institutions like government and global NGOs.

We worked with Samsung in more than thirty different studies over a decade to understand the emergence of the smartphone and its impact on society; we partnered with Intel for ten years to look at how "computers" (PCs) were shifting to "computing" (the cloud), helping direct a major chip manufacturer's initiatives. When local foods and flavor profiles spread across the globe, we studied how it worked and what it all meant. We partnered with pharmaceutical companies in far-flung corners of the globe to investigate why people weren't taking their medicine and why so many communities exhibited vaccine hesitancy. We sent our researchers to the Middle East to understand radical Islam in the Muslim Brotherhood and created the brands for the tourist boards of Greenland and Denmark. We went deep into the communities organized to commit credit card fraud on a mass scale, and we lived with QAnon conspiracy theorists to understand beliefs like the flat-earth theory and Holocaust deniers. During this time, we worked with the world's largest companies, names like Ford, Chanel, Lego, and Adidas, and watched the world of fashion turn upside down, cars go electric, toys go digital, and sports change radically.

In our quest, we often played a contrarian role. Over the years, different trends around creativity and innovation have come and gone. Sometimes they involved Post-it notes, workshops, and "blue sky" thinking where everyone was supposed to weigh in. Other times they involved experts, trendspotters, and other priests of creativity who used divination tools to discern creative trends from on high.

Our work at ReD cut through all of this by showing our clients that the creativity bandwagon was a red herring. When you arrive at meaningful insights about a phenomenon, it's easy to imagine products and services that will feel relevant for people. Creativity is never radical, insights are.

At ReD Associates, we didn't invent any new methodology. We used the observational practices in this book. Each partner of the firm took these practices and used our platform to do the work they wanted, to ask the questions that kept them up at night, to follow their own obsessions. That freedom was precisely what our company was built for in the first place.

Get out and find a Looking Lab that inspires you or make one up yourself. Make sure that the people who invest in you get great returns. Start with observation always. Don't think, look.

OBSERVING NORMAL AND MARGINAL PRACTICES

Why on Earth Would People Subscribe to Cable?

We persuaded several American and European telecom companies, new technology firms coming out of Silicon Valley as well as a colossal manufacturer of TVs, to fund a series of projects to understand this phenomenon. To study the future of technology as it relates to human practice, you need techniques and perspectives to guide you, or you get lost. There is so much out there—so many things happening— what is relevant and what is noise? To disclose a new world of media and media consumption, we used a method we called "Normal and Marginal Practices."

This was how, in the early aughts, I found myself immersed in observational data from a subculture engaging in a "marginal practice," in Okinawa, Japan. Marginal practices are behaviors that occur outside the norm of social practices for the phenomenon. In 2004, it was normal to use a remote control to watch a cable subscription package or whatever show was playing on network TV. What was not normal, decidedly marginal, was the shared social practice of a tiny group of people in a Japanese city who all had an interest in movies and TV shows shot in Monument Valley in northeast Arizona. Films like John Ford's *Stagecoach* and Stanley Kubrick's *2001: A Space Odyssey* have all been shot in this vast valley because of its moonlike buttes. The group in Okinawa did not share other similarities—some were old, some young, some wore ties and worked professional "salary" jobs, while others were slackers watching from their childhood bedrooms. The obsession uniting all of them was an interest in finding media shot in this setting. That seemed to be a highly specific micro-obsession. In a time of early internet access and limited social media, they went to inordinate lengths to get it. The groups would have multiyear conversations about where to access the articles, documentaries, and movies they were seeking on Monument Valley. They shared digitized versions of old VHS recordings with terrible sound, and they did their best to connect with other Monument Valley aficionados all over the world through early social media sites like Friendster. Monument Valley friends would follow each other's lives without ever having met by keeping in touch in chat rooms and on platforms like Reddit and the WELL.

The subculture in Okinawa would watch their movies for hours together and talk to each other online and on text while watching. Often, several of them would huddle together around two PC screens. One PC screen showed the movie while the second PC screen was kept open for a discussion about what they were watching in a highly detailed and specific language difficult for outsiders to decipher.

The group in Okinawa led us to hundreds of other communities displaying this marginal practice all over the world—from suburban basements in Montana, to dorm rooms in South Korea, Lagos, and Austin, to watch parties with lawyers and executives in cosmopolitan cities all over the world—each group was looking for different material to watch but exhibiting the same patterns of behavior. These were groups organized around micro-interests, and they were hunting all around the globe for their increasingly specialized interests. This came to be called "content"—not files or TV—and it included movies, articles, and videos. That word *content* sounded odd, important somehow. We intuited that "content" might be a hook into a larger story—a collapse of all forms of watching into one word—a gestalt shift waiting to happen.

It was clear that cable television, and the more conventional behavior around television watching, wasn't giving these communities what they were seeking, so many of them were turning to a marginal practice of illegal downloading. Napster had already created havoc in the music industry by giving users access to IP-protected media, so BitTorrent sites that helped users download and upload files were not the innovation here. Torrents were simply the only platforms offering these subcultures the content they really wanted. They would gladly have paid for the media they used, but that wasn't possible. Their cable subscriptions just didn't have anything to offer. They had to steal it. When we observed our respondents access new illegal downloads, we noted the emergence of the marginal practice that would come to be known as "binge-watching." They wouldn't just watch the latest episode of their favorite show once a week but would have marathon screenings globally for hours on end. Years later Netflix would popularize this behavior by releasing all episodes of a show at once.

Across four continents, we spent months looking at this asynchronous media consumption: How did tens of thousands of people find ways to organize vast amounts of media files on thousands of host servers to create the media they wanted to see? We found super-local communities emerging on the internet where micro-celebrities would target a tiny sliver of people in each country. Within these marginal practices, some of these micro-celebrities started blogs or created a series of small video clips. Today we would call them online influencers, YouTubers, or content creators, but at the time, the phenomenon was new. Each celebrity garnered only a small audience, but when added up globally, a new business model for media writ large was made possible.

While following the bread crumbs of these global microcommunities, we found other evidence of what seemed like new behavior. The people inventing and embracing these new forms of media use rarely used their TV sets. Many had large TV sets but would mostly interact with media on smaller laptop screens. The quality of the screen and particularly the sound was much lower than the TV set in the room next door. But the media community they were part of was simply not accessible on the big screen. They also didn't seem to mind. It was clear to us that if these behaviors went mainstream, someone needed to warn the TV manufacturers and cable companies.

We ended up calling what we found "Social TV," a new kind of TV without geographical roots and asynchronous—but deeply social in nature.

The crucial methodological move when you try to study the marginal and the experimental is to stick to the phenomenon (in this case, the remote control) and not get carried away with everything you observe. Not every exciting new experimental practice is a key to change and the future. It is the combination of observing and understanding the marginal with an awareness of what is typical and average every day for most people that matters. The normal is as vital as the new. If all you do is hunt down the strange and weird, you will never understand what might happen. But when you combine the new with the normal, you can bet on what will most likely become the norm in the future.

The most important marginal behavior we observed was the phenomenon of asynchronous media consumption, or streaming content not according to a cable or television network timetable but on a schedule that suited the individual watchers. At the time, in 2004, this behavior was far below the radar of executives of the largest media companies in the world. Cable and satellite subscriptions were still too lucrative, and TV manufacturers still designed their products to serve those subscriptions. Our observations showed us that streaming would turn the media world on its head in the following twenty years. We advised our clients to get ready for new consumption patterns that would change the world of news, sports, and national media for all of us. We built new kinds of services into mass-market TVs and moved huge budgets to new product development in streaming and highly specialized micro-media.

Today we know that some podcasts—produced with only two microphones and a laptop—have more listeners and viewers in a single episode than an entire week of content created by CNN. The twenty-first-century media company now consists of highly specialized media on different online platforms like YouTube and Twitch. It is already replacing the media institutions of the twentieth century.

By studying the pockets of media behavior that pointed in the direction of future practices, we could help predict a future that was already happening in the present.

LEARNING TO SEE THE FUTURE IN TODAY

The writer William Gibson is known for his remark that the future is already here—just unevenly distributed. The future can be found in just these pockets around the world where marginal practices are already creating behavior everyone will be doing five or ten years from now. To figure out what might happen to an industry or any part of our human world, carefully observing and even participating in these marginal practices can be a portal to understanding what comes next.

Gibson and other science fiction authors already know this. They will tell you that the source of inspiration for their work is rarely musings about the future but, instead, observations about existing competing futures that are happening now. This gaze or perspective is clarifying. To observe these futures, it's helpful to think about what people in ten years would say about what you are seeing today.

This science fiction or time-travel speculation technique can help when sorting through empirical observations of hundreds of people worldwide. Often the future is blatantly obvious when you combine the dual lenses of marginal practice and then imagine which practice will look normal and everyday as seen from the future. Speculation like this always needs to be grounded in empirical observation and evidence gathering. Otherwise, it veers off into trend-talk nonsense, often referred to as "thought leadership," "futuring," or "scenario planning." Without a process of direct observation, all of these practices are just hyperbole.

When studying any practice or relationship to a phenomenon in a particular geographical place, separating what is a universal behavior and what is a specific behavior to the site and groups of people you are observing is necessary. When you are, as we were, working at a global scale, you need to generalize. The TV sets, cars, or online services we needed to help make and change were designed for a worldwide market, and there was no way they would individuate for each culture or country. People have different ways of watching television depending on the local culture; we call those particulars. But it is also necessary and possible to extract shared reasons for consuming or making media content that cut across all cultures; we call those universals. People are different and have roots in meaningful differences in where they live and work, but it is surprising how many universal practices we all have and share. It is impossible to make anything for a global market without separating universals and particulars. And because most of our clients were among the largest companies in the world, we needed to balance how to differentiate for local cultures and when to lean in to our common humanity and sociology.

To my surprise, the clients we worked with over time always told us that they had difficulty wrapping their heads around any kind of meaningful change. To defend their market position, taking risks is not always rewarded. Budgets for thinking about change and the future are significant but not nearly enough relative to their importance. Some of the companies we worked with needed to be dragged into the future. There is nothing wrong with that, but in my experience, people tend to underestimate how much can and will change in our everyday lives.

If you had told me five years ago, for example, that the entire world would be shut down because of a virus coming out of a fish market in

Wuhan, I probably would have rolled my eyes. The idea that we would run global companies from our home offices and bedrooms would have seemed ludicrous. Yet we did and still do. If someone had told me twenty years ago that everyone alive would have a small rectangular piece of glass in their pockets that gave access to all the information ever collected and a way to talk to anyone in the world, I would also have been skeptical. In my childhood, the galvanizing idea the environmental movement rallied around was opposition to nuclear energy. But had someone told the members of that movement in 1989 that in only thirty years, they would end up seeing nuclear energy as a positive and reasonable idea to address human-made changes to the weather and fossil fuels controlled by countries run by despots, they never would have believed it.

Change—radical change—that would be incomprehensible just a few years ago happens all the time. Even the most profound and most basic ideas about what it means to be human have changed. Not long ago—and still for many of us—being human meant being God's children. The world was created around us, and we answered to God. Now we think differently about something as basic as our own humanity. To be human is to be an animal, blurring the line between human and nature. Machines used to be a mechanical extension of us. But within the past ten years, machines have started to share many of our characteristics (like pattern recognition and some forms of creativity). It isn't apparent anymore what separates us from the rest of nature and makes us different from machines. Historian of science Thomas Kuhn famously called these changes to our understanding of the universe, nature, and our place in it "paradigm shifts." When one paradigm replaces another, the old seems to be from another time.

Considering this, it shouldn't come as a surprise that the world constantly changes in deep and meaningful ways. But it is nearly always remarkable how it happens. As Ernesto Laclau told us, "Change happens like a thief in the night." Major dislocations in how we experience the world seem obvious two minutes after they happen. The day we got our first smartphone, our old flip phone became a strange artifact from a distant past. It seems incomprehensible how life was before FaceTime or Google Maps. How on earth did we coordinate anything or get anywhere? Humans adapt instantly to change but often without understanding the long-term consequences. At ReD, we tried to keep this radical openness to the transformation of even the most profound and philosophical questions as part of all projects. The future is never a theoretical prospect for any of us. You can observe it in your everyday reality. The most challenging thing for all of us to see is what is really there.

EVERYTHING YOU NEED TO
KNOW BEGINS WITH BIRDS

At a low moment on a dreary February day several years ago, we reached an impasse on a challenging project in our ReD offices. Thick sleet fell in clumps outside our windows. Even the pigeons looked depressed.

No one on our project team had an inspiring idea about where to look next, so we sat around our worktable in inert silence, some looking out the window, some scribbling aimlessly in notebooks. It was at just that moment that one of our researchers, Jonathan, came into our conference room and placed a slim paperback book on the table.

"I know we are under a deadline," he told all of us, "but first we need to take a quick break and read this book."

The elegant book he put in front of all of us had a drawing of a falcon on it, and the title announced *The Peregrine*. In the 1960s—more than fifty years ago—no one had ever heard of it. It was not an auspicious beginning.

"I don't think any of us will ever find a better guide for how to do observational work," Jonathan told us.

Because I take a recommendation like that very seriously—and because we needed to look at something other than participant interviews and fieldwork notes—I ordered copies for the entire team. We took our heads out of our observational data for a pause to consider the strange book before us on the table.

When we all returned to that project at ReD, everyone who had read *The Peregrine* was a changed person. Many of us still cite it as one of the most important books on observation ever written. I found it so inspiring that I made it the anchor in my course on human observation. Despite their surprise at seeing the old-fashioned cover at the beginning of class, my students always tell me that it is the most important reading in the entire semester. Often they end up giving the book to friends and family, and there is a run on *The Peregrine* stock at the Strand bookstore close to the school. It is simply the best book I have ever come by to explain what masterful observation is and how it works. Go buy it, read it, and learn it by heart.

How did this one slender volume about an eccentric British bird watcher change my own practice—as well as the practice of so many of the best observers in the world? Let's start at the beginning.

The writer behind *The Peregrine*, J. A. Baker, is a mysterious character. Until his biography was published in 2017, little was known about the British man who obsessively tracked peregrine falcons across the flatlands and marshes of Essex for ten years. He took fastidious notes while tracking peregrine falcons over the course of a decade across the desolate estuaries of the East Anglian coast, and these direct observations form the foundation for the poetic nature writing that appears in *The Peregrine*. The book follows an unnamed narrator across a single winter while he tracks migrant peregrine falcons. During this time, he tells us that he observes a particular tiercel, a male peregrine, and a relationship develops between the two of them. The book explores his observations of the falcons—the tiercel specifically—as well as the changes he experiences within himself as his obsession with watching them overcomes him.

When he published the book in 1967, many in the world of nature writing were stunned by its strangeness. It was unlike any other nature writing before it—wholly distinctive in its vision of the symbiosis that occurs between an observer and the observed. This care between Baker and his tiercel—one might even call it a kind of love—fuels his desire to subsume his entire being into the life and body of the bird. "Science can never be enough," Baker wrote of his unique approach in his writing. "Emotion and sentiment will always rule."

Who was Baker as a person? After *The Peregrine* was published to great acclaim—it won the 1967 Duff Cooper Memorial Prize and *Yorkshire Post*'s book of the year—editors, reporters, and fans sought him out, and journalists gave him the moniker "the man who thinks like a hawk." *The Sunday Times* ran the only piece that offered a tidbit of information—and even this only a tease:

> John Baker is 40 and lives in a council flat in Essex. He doesn't want it known which town. He doesn't want his neighbours to know what he does. He hasn't got a phone or a TV. He never goes anywhere socially and the last time he went out to be entertained was 12 years ago when he went to the pictures to see Shane.

The real John Baker wrote only one other book, *The Hill of Summer*, and it suffered in comparison with the eccentric brilliance of *The Peregrine*. He continued to live a quiet life with his wife, Doreen, in their council flat until his death from cancer in 1987. His masterpiece was out of print and almost forgotten when a new generation of writers, naturalists, filmmakers, and environmentalists discovered it. Whether they know it or not, *The Peregrine* has now informed the strategic outlook of many of the world's most powerful companies. Everything you need to know about hyper-reflection is contained right there within its pages.

LESSON ONE: LEARN TO SEE WHAT IS REALLY THERE

Baker's first lesson for all of us was in the opening to *The Peregrine*. "The hardest thing of all to see," he says, "is what is really there."

> Books about birds show pictures of the peregrine, and the text is full of information. Large and isolated in the gleaming whiteness of the page, the hawk stares back at you, bold, statuesque, brightly colored. But when you have shut the book, you will never see that bird again.

For Baker, learning to see the falcon had nothing to do with what he called the "close and static image." Instead, Baker set out to see what was there. This is because he had no interest in observing nature from a detached position behind the glass of a museum case or a pair of binoculars. The bird he was training himself to see was not an intellectual conceit; it was a living thing.

"The living bird will never be so large, so shiny-bright," he tells us. "It will be deep in landscape, and always sinking farther back, always at the point of being lost. Pictures are waxworks beside the passionate mobility of the living bird."

What you are observing, in other words, is your own state of expectation. You are always at the edge of not seeing anything at all. Reality—whether it be a living bird or any other phenomenon—will not present itself to you in a tidy framework or a neat matrix of ideas. That which is worth observing, life itself, Baker reminds us, is close to imperceptible, barely a shimmer of movement in the grass or a sound far in the distance. If we don't cultivate enough patience and fortitude to be sensitive enough to see life as it is really lived, we will miss it all.

LESSON TWO: OBSERVATION
HINGES ON OBSESSION

Once you have started to observe a phenomenon, you must find yourself obsessed by it, or the observations will be of little value. When I say *obsessed*, I mean driven to see the phenomenon in its every form. Only then will you discover the full complexity of how it hides itself and what its revelations hold.

Baker has a beautiful way of describing this compulsive drive. He tells us that he spent a decade searching for the "restless brilliance" of that first peregrine, a falcon with an extraordinary "fire of spirit."

> For ten years I have been looking upward for that cloud-biting anchor shape, that crossbow flinging through the air. The eye becomes insatiable for hawks. It clicks towards them with ecstatic fury, just as the hawk's eye swings and dilates to the lurid food-shapes of gulls and pigeons.

What is it you are looking for? What is the human behavior you are trying to understand? Unless your "eye becomes insatiable for hawks," you will miss it. It will disguise itself in myriad ways and, without obsession, you will not have considered its shape shifting outside of your preconceptions and misguided assumptions. You want your eye to "click towards" your chosen observation with "ecstatic fury." With anything less, you will not be able to recognize the object of your obsession in all its inchoate forms.

Let your eye become insatiable for the phenomenon. Suddenly, you will see it—like the "cloud-biting anchor shape"—everywhere you look. Hidden in plain sight—what is really there.

LESSON THREE: GOOD OBSERVATIONS ALWAYS INCLUDE THE OBSERVER

Baker is straightforward with his project. He will not leave himself out of the frame. It is his care that is creating the observation, so we must know just as much about how and why he cares as we know about the falcon.

> In my diary of a single winter I have tried to preserve a unity, binding together the bird, the watcher, and the place that holds them both. Everything I describe took place while I was watching it, but I do not believe that honest observation is enough. The emotions and behaviour of the watcher are also facts, and they must be truthfully recorded.

Just as the gestalt theorists showed us, Baker cannot observe the foreground of the peregrine falcon without also observing the background of the world the falcon inhabits. He himself is a part of that background. Baker is part of the whole. The watcher, through the act of watching, is in the middle of the phenomenon, not standing outside.

LESSON FOUR: OBSERVATIONS ARE NOT OPINIONS

When you go out into the world and observe, you are not in the business of forming opinions: Your only job is to accurately describe the phenomenon. Instead of opining or jumping first into ideology, focus on direct observation. See what is so hard to see—what is really there—and the mysteries that unfold behind life's daily practices.

Consider Baker's acutely observed description of the peregrine's kills. Instead of resorting to opining with sentimental anthropomorphic conceits, Baker illustrates the power of simple, clean description.

> I shall try to make plain the bloodiness of killing. . . . All birds eat living flesh at some time in their lives. Consider the cold-eyed thrush, that springy carnivore of lawns, worm stabber, basher to death of snails. We should not sentimentalise his song, and forget the killing that sustains it.

When we set out to observe, we want to scrape away the residue of cliché and received opinion. Stop thinking. Observation is not an intellectual pursuit; it is an embodied presence. Wait, watch, describe: "The hawk's foot reached out, and gripped, and squeezed, and quenched the dunlin's heart as effortlessly as a man's finger extinguishing an insect."

Great observers are not boosters, advocates, or PR agents. We argue only for truth.

LESSON FIVE: OBSERVATION BEGINS
WITH SYSTEMATIC WATCHING

Throughout his adult life, Baker developed a process with his bird-watching he called "systematic watching." Over his many years of exploring the same salt tides and estuaries, he kept fastidious field books and notes on the birds he observed. In these notes, the material he later shaped into *The Peregrine*, he included facts and numbers of all types. He records that in ten winters, he found "619 peregrine kills" and includes a list of those species represented, including 38 percent wood pigeon and 14 percent black-headed gull.

It is in these lists of facts and figures—and others throughout the book—that we see Baker's fastidious systems for observation. Put simply, he is doing his homework. He is noticing, watching, and recording what he sees. He learns the names of birds and animals to identify them. A bat is not just a bat but a particular kind of bat, a "pipistrelle." A crow is not just a crow but a "jackdaw" or a "rook." Without becoming an ornithologist or an ecologist, he has developed a deep understanding of their core vocabulary.

He quantifies only to reveal context. So when we learn about the weight of the falcon's eyes—"approximately one ounce each"—it is in relation to the human eye. "If our eyes were in the same proportion to our bodies as the peregrine's are to his, a twelve stone man would have eyes three inches across, weighing four pounds."

This systematic watching enables him to begin observing the hawk through the changing nature of the rest of the context. He learns to see a falcon through the movement of the other birds in relation to it.

In this way, the invisible is made visible. "When hawks have gone from sight, you must look up into the sky," Baker tells us. "Their reflection rises in the birds that fear them. There is so much more sky than land."

The thorough nature of his systematic watching enables him to draw insightful conclusions from the empirical data he has collected: "These tables suggest that the juvenile peregrine preys mainly on those species that are most numerous in its hunting territory, provided they weigh at least half a pound."

Eventually he ventures an assertion based only on that which he has observed with his own eyes: "Predators that kill what is commonest have the best chance of survival. Those that develop a preference for one species only are more likely to go hungry and to succumb to disease." Notice how he doesn't lean any more in to theory. He doesn't use this small conclusive assertion as a stepping stone to something bigger and more abstract—beyond the scope of his own human eye. Before an observer can do anything else, he shows us, we gather as much data as possible from clean observation.

LESSON SIX: THE MOOD MATTERS

Baker knows his context intimately—the estuaries, the fields, and the wet, musty salt marshes—so that even his observations of other creatures beyond the falcon convey a mood. He is attuned to the relationship that exists between himself and the falcon, between the falcon and its prey, and between other creatures and their predators. The more Baker's narrator absorbs the perspective of the hawk, the more he can move fluidly into the "as if" space of the other creatures within the hawk's ecosystem.

LESSON SEVEN: WORK LIKE A BIRD

Just as great observers absorb the mood and the aesthetics of their subjects, they also develop a sensitivity for their integrity. This has nothing to do with whether subjects are good, just, or greedy. Just as opinions have no place here, morality is also beside the point—lifted straight from the world of humans. Instead, this sensitivity is an appreciation for how a falcon lives up to its fullest ideal.

As Baker learned, the peregrine spends most of the morning in a kind of meditative state of preparation. To be a brilliant hunter, Baker tells us, is to first put oneself in a state of heightened awareness. "The hawk rouses only gradually from his post-bathing lethargy," and "his first flights are short and unhurried." The falcon "moves from perch to perch, watching other birds and occasionally catching an insect or a mouse on the ground."

The morning doesn't appear to be productive in our conventional understanding of the word. Instead, it is a state of relaxation that gives way to a more structured practice period and what we might call "warming up." The falcon "reenacts the whole process of learning to kill that he went through when he first left the eyrie."

In this careful attention to the structured days of the peregrine, the narrator is learning his own lessons of the hunting life. Great hunters spend most of their time absorbing the context of what they hope to hunt. This involves imaginative exercises—play—as Baker observes in the behavior of the falcons. The hawk may "feint at partridges, harass jackdaws or lapwings, skirmish with crows." Killing can also be accidental as this play becomes unexpectedly violent.

"Afterwards he seems baffled by what he has done, and he may leave the kill where it fell and return to it later when he is genuinely hunting."

Hunger drives the actual hunt and kill, but in reality, this is a very small part of the falcon's day. Baker observes this and finds an admirable economy in this approach to life. "When an attack is made, it is usually a single vicious stoop." This spectacular show of violence is mere minutes in the falcon's day. All too often we humans push papers, ideas, or money around at a monotonous pace with no time for rest and even less time to stay receptive to a glorious moment of insight. The pace of our days and the meaning that exists inside of them suffers in comparison with those of the falcon. Work like a bird.

LESSON EIGHT:
PERCEIVE WITH THE EYES OF A HAWK

The most skilled anthropologists argue that observation is never sufficient until you can see the ghosts of others. The observer goes from the systematic watching that creates a deep knowledge and empathic engagement to, ultimately, an act of symbiosis. Their ghosts are your ghosts. When you have given yourself over fully to the act of observation, you must allow for self-transformation.

The best observations change you. It is a metamorphosis to understand the bodily experience of another—whether human or animal. What does the world look like through the eyes of a falcon? What does he see when he wakes up in the morning? What does he feel driven to do and why?

Baker begins his journey with how and what the hawk sees. His approach utilizes scientific details as a launchpad for imagination. "The whole retina of a hawk's eye," he tells us, "records a resolution of distant objects that is twice as acute as that of the human retina."

Quantified observations like "twice as acute" create stepping stones from research and direct observation into an intuitive and imaginative understanding of the hawk's lived experience: "This means that a hawk, endlessly scanning the landscape with small abrupt turns of his head, will pick up any point of movement; by focussing upon it he can immediately make it flare up into larger, clearer view."

This is analytical empathy: the essential ingredient for observation at its finest. It allows Baker to occupy even more of an imaginative space based on his deep knowledge of the falcon. Over time, he no longer notes what he sees the hawk doing; instead, he begins to place himself in the perspective of the hawk. He starts by asking questions about this perspective. What is it like to be you? In Baker's questioning, we see a meticulous attention to the experience of perception. What does the falcon experience when man appears? Does the falcon have size constancy? Does the falcon know where its wing is flapping in the wind? How does the falcon experience fear, dread, glory? Tremendous insights are available to those who obsessively observe and attempt to experience the world through another's body. *What is it really like to be you?*

LESSON NINE: OBSERVATION MUST BE DONE WITH THE ETHICS OF CHARACTER

If you have any hope of achieving meaningful observation, you must consider what is appropriate within the world you are observing. As Aristotle argues in book two of *The Nicomachean Ethics*, ethics of character guide one to do the right thing, at the right time, and in the right way. This is how Baker approaches his role. Instead of inserting himself into the context of the falcon with the arrogance that his ways are superior, he seeks out recognition and acceptance of the hawk on its own terms. He carefully considers what is appropriate, and he adjusts his behavior accordingly: "You must wear the same clothes, travel by the same way, perform actions in the same order."

This includes practical ideas that account for the bird's fear of unpredictability. "Enter and leave the same fields at the same time each day, soothe the hawk from its wildness by a ritual of behaviour as invariable as its own," and "let your shape grow in size but do not alter its outline." The narrator has directly observed his tiercel enough to assert that "a peregrine fears nothing he can see clearly and far off."

These are straightforward and practical suggestions that any observer can use. Baker, however, has an even more poetic approach to what character might look like to his tiercel. What is the right thing, at the right time, and in the right way to a hawk? "Shun the furtive oddity of man," he tells us. "To share fear is the greatest bond of all." If an observer has any hope of seeing something meaningful, transcendence is necessary and must be absolute. "The hunter must become the thing he hunts."

What is appropriate is nothing less than a rebirth. The narrator helps us understand the contraction of the two perspectives between the watcher and the watched, or the hunter and the hunted. Baker shifts into using *we* to signify the transformation that occurs. He is now the falcon: "We live, in these days in the open, the same ecstatic fearful life."

It is in this transformation of perception that all character reveals itself. Is one willing to forgo all of one's assumptions and habits of thought to fully embody the lived experience of another? When one acts with the ethics of character in the world of the peregrine, "a vivid sense of place grows like another limb," and "direction has colour and meaning." It is the only appropriate action for this place and time.

OBSERVATION TAKES TIME

We started our journey toward an observational practice with the basic building blocks of perception. How do we see a white dot on a white piece of paper? Where do we stand when we want to look at a painting? What does our body do to navigate around other people on the street and in a coffee shop? These questions, seemingly simple, gave us the foundation for creating a precise understanding of how perception works.

With a grounding in this philosophy firmly in place, I sent you, like my students, out into the world to do direct observation. As you may already be discovering, this kind of observation can take place anywhere and everywhere—at work, on the streets, in your favorite bar, or at a conference or retreat. The most important thing to remember is to keep turning your attention back to "the thing itself." What is the human phenomenon you are trying to understand? Based on what do people do what they do? With practice and patience, new understanding will almost always emerge.

In addition to all the observational skills I have shared with you, I now encourage you to cultivate patience. This act of "looking" is the most productive way you can spend any day. At times, however, it will not feel that way. You won't be checking off boxes, responding to emails, or sitting in meetings chasing down new clients or strategizing new futures. What you will be doing, however—observing the world with an insatiable curiosity about human behavior—will take you much, much further than any red herring of productivity. This is because all activity is meaningless if you don't have an actual insight to guide your efforts.

Give yourself time. Any worthwhile observation process is slow, singular, and nonlinear. You cannot follow a five-point plan, and you will not work like a scientist. You will bring your own peculiarities to the process—along with an awareness of them—and you will have to grow comfortable with doubting and drifting. Just like Franz Boas or my student Avinash, you might find yourself disoriented and seeking out a more efficient model. Maybe, like Gillian Tett, you will discover things that are unpopular and against the grain. Don't fall for a framework, an easy answer, or the herd mentality just to ease your own uncertainty. Ensure that you have the freedom—the time and the space—to say, "I don't know." And then try to look around and find out.

The reward for all this discomfort is twofold. First, you will begin to think for yourself. Instead of absorbing other people's analyses and opinions or jumping on the bandwagon with trendy answers to complex phenomena you don't understand, you will cultivate an independent mind. You will develop the ability to enter a room anywhere at any time with the confidence to say, "I don't know," and the skills to find out.

This kind of independent thinking is the source of all insight. Insights don't come with every problem, and they certainly don't come every day, but sometimes you will get lucky and arrive at a moment of profound understanding. I often refer to this experience as a "moment of clarity." All the data suddenly lines up, and a general story emerges from it. I liken it to the experience of walking through a planned forest. At first, it appears as if the trees are chaotically placed, and the perspective feels disorienting. Suddenly, however, when you shift yourself at just the right angle, you realize that the trees are organized in patterns and rows. Every one of them lines up to create a satisfying vista of unity. The entire forest snaps from chaos into order, and everything you see makes sense.

When you experience an insight like this—especially after having wrestled with a particular topic for a long period of time—it is a tremendous relief. The truth of reality emerges from the patterns of the phenomenon. Your mind is finally at ease. The experience of this kind of insight is so thrilling, in fact, it justifies all the effort. It could be an end in and of itself.

There is, however, a second benefit to the practice that, for some of you, might prove even more valuable. Insights are the necessary platform for any worthwhile invention or innovation. Once you begin to have insights, you immediately recognize that coming up with new ideas, technologies, or solutions has very little to do with creativity. Instead, everything starts with the insight, and what follows is logical and obvious given what an insight has revealed to you. Innovation and invention are all possible—inevitable, really—once you arrive at the insight.

I've seen groups, firms, and leaders attempt to reverse these two: begin with a process of innovation and use it to arrive at an insight about human behavior. It never works. In all my time observing, I have never encountered a single meaningful innovation that did not come from a deep insight into human behavior. You don't need to hire creativity experts, fill Post-it notes with brainstorms, or gather for team-building exercises in thought leadership. Time is precious: don't waste it coming up with ideas or solutions detached from a meaningful human world. Any process that begins with creativity, rather than an insight, is doomed to fail.

Use the words of J. A. Baker in *The Peregrine* to inspire you: work like a bird. The falcon spends most of its days in a meditative preparation for brief and intense periods of activity. Instead of using your time to chase after myths about how creativity works, do some direct observation. Immerse yourself in the context of what you hope to understand. Whether you want to know about breakthroughs in artificial intelligence, make more thoughtful decisions around climate change, move toward a plant-based diet, or simply try to be more attentive to your own family, start not with action but with a passive state of reception. Talk less, look more. Pay attention; wait, watch. And use your own sense of care to guide you. Just like Baker's bird watcher, you have the potential for transformation through this practice, but you must care about what you are seeing.

When I say *care*, I don't mean you have to love it, admire it, or even find it ethical. I just mean you must find it fascinating—worthy of your most obsessive eye. This might mean it disappoints you—the source of all great philosophy—or even that it breaks your heart. It just needs to be of abiding interest to you as a human phenomenon.

Only then, when your eye is compelled to see it in all its myriad shapes and forms, will you understand what you can do about it.

So now, I send you out into the world to look around. Everything you need to know is already out there just waiting for you to see it. It will take time, but you'll soon find it's worth it. Leave your calendar free and unscheduled. Listen for the social silence. Wait for what matters most in the world: a moment of insight.

After an insight, everything else is possible. Inevitable really.

ACKNOWLEDGMENTS

The Great Simon Critchley helped me design the courses this book covers from start to finish. You gave me philosophical safety and permitted me to push my interpretations of the material way beyond what exists today. Thanks, mate. YNWA.

Without my students, I wouldn't have found all the subtleties in the phenomenon of human observation. Many of the students taking the course went to extremes to observe and learn, even when uncomfortable or borderline unsafe. Thank you. It was fun and thrilling.

Professor Taylor Carman helped me understand Maurice Merleau-Ponty in a way that made the dense text come alive and gave me many examples that made the philosophy sink in.

My partners at ReD Associates helped me get my arms around the skill of observation through hundreds of projects in every corner of the world: Mikkel Rasmussen, Filip Lau, Jun Lee, Michele Chang,

Sandra Cariglio, Mikkel Krenckel, Millie Arora, and Charlotte Vangsgaard, among many others.

Caitlin Murray from the Judd Foundation in Marfa helped me see the whole of Judd's world—including his library. Seth Cameron helped me understand the perception of color. Gil Ash connected me to the highly specialized world of clay and skeet shooting and the innovation he represents. A bomb went off in my head when I learned about how much perception, new findings in neuroscience, and relative velocity are connected. Gillian Tett helped me connect the theory of Bourdieu to the world of journalism.

Jonathan Lowndes introduced me to *The Peregrine* and other key texts that were seminal for me.

Andrew Zuckerman has been my writing idol and inspired the writing to be lush.

Ann Marie Healy for helping me straighten out and enrich my thoughts and writing and for making me laugh.

Jake Morrissey and the entire team at Riverhead for supporting this project from the beginning and providing indefatigable editorial guidance. Thank you for believing in a book on Merleau-Ponty.

Zoë Pagnamenta for serving as my agent throughout every one of my projects. No one knows the world of books better.

NOTES

THE MAGIC OF PERCEPTION

23 **so the story goes:** Sarah Bakewell, *At the Existential Café: Freedom, Being, and Apricot Cocktails* (New York: Other Press, 2017).

THE FIRST LOOKING LAB: THE STORY OF GESTALT

27 **hopped on a train in Vienna:** Edwin B. Newman, "Max Wertheimer: 1880–1943," *American Journal of Psychology* 57, no. 3 (July 1944): 428–35.

29 **the speed of mental processes:** David K. Robinson, "Reaction-Time Experiments in Wundt's Institute and Beyond," in *Wilhelm Wundt in History: The Making of a Scientific Psychology*, ed. Robert W. Rieber and David K. Robinson (Kluwer Academic/Plenum Publishers, 2001), 161–204.

29 **his lab in Leipzig:** Serge Nicolas and Ludovic Ferrand, "Wundt's Laboratory at Leipzig in 1891," *History of Psychology* 2, no. 3 (August 1999): 194–203.

30 **love of hiking:** Carl Stumpf, "Autobiography of Carl Stumpf," in *History of Psychology in Autobiography*, vol. 1, ed. Carl Murchison (Russell & Russell, 1930), 389–441.

31 **collection of the earliest recordings:** Phonogramm-Archiv (Berlin) ("phonogram archive"): Carl Stumpf and Erich Moritz von Hornbostel, founders, 1900, soundandscience.de/location/phonogramm-archiv-berlin.

31 **music of the Vedda singers:** Michael Wertheimer, "Music, Thinking, Perceived Motion: The Emergence of Gestalt Theory," *History of Psychology* 17, no. 2 (2014): 131–33.

32 **There is, Ehrenfels suggested:** Christian von Ehrenfels, "On Gestalt Quali-
ties," in *Foundations of Gestalt Theory*, ed. and trans. Barry Smith (Philosophia Verlag,
1988), 82–117.

33 **in experimental psychology, Sigmund Exner:** Edwin G. Boring, *Sensation and
Perception in the History of Experimental Psychology* (New York: D. Appleton-Century,
1942), 594.

33 **train conductor called out:** The story I tell here is an imaginative exercise
helping to give more of a narrative to comments Max Wertheimer shared with
his colleagues. I want to give a special acknowledgment to Michael Wertheimer
and D. Brett King for inspiring this retelling with their historical biography *Max
Wertheimer and Gestalt Theory* (London: Routledge, Taylor and Francis Group,
2005).

35 **Köhler wrote after meeting:** Wolfgang Köhler, "Gestalt Psychology," in
The Selected Papers of Wolfgang Kohler, ed. Mary Henle (New York: Liveright, 1971),
108–22.

37 **figures in motion:** D. Brett King and Michael Wertheimer, *Max Wertheimer and
Gestalt Theory* (London: Routledge, Taylor and Francis Group, 2005), 100.

38 **"[The wholes] are in no way":** Kurt Koffka, "Perception: An Introduction to the
Gestalt-theorie," first published in *Psychological Bulletin* 19 (1922): 531–85, psychclassics
.yorku.ca/Koffka/Perception/perception.htm.

38 **"On or about December 1910":** Will Hodgkinson, "Culture Quake: The Post
Impressionist Exhibition, 1910," May 25, 2016, last modified January 17, 2023,
bl.uk/20th-century-literature/articles/culture-quake-the-post-impressionist-
exhibition-1910.

39 **It was April 15, 1874:** Ulrike Becks-Malorny, *Cezanne* (New York: Taschen, 1995),
28.

40 **one of their cohort, Édouard Manet:** Becks-Malorny, *Cezanne*, 45.

41 **"wallpaper in its embryonic state":** *Impression* magazine, "Impressionists: From
Scorn to Stardom," October 10, 2020, last modified January 17, 2023, impression
-magazine.com/history-of-impressionism/.

41 **"bricklayer who paints with his trowel":** Becks-Malorny, *Cezanne*, 28.

42 **"You must think":** Becks-Malorny, *Cezanne*, 46.

42 **"The reforming process":** Becks-Malorny, *Cezanne*, 48.

44 **landscape of his childhood home:** Becks-Malorny, *Cezanne*, 67–79.

THREE ARTISTS: HOW TO SEE BEYOND
CONVENTION AND CLICHÉ

63 **"Most art is fragile":** Donald Judd, "Statement for the Chinati Foundation,"
1987, quoted on Chinati website, last modified January 17, 2023, chinati.org/about
/mission-history/.

67   **"The thing, as a whole"**: Donald Judd, "Specific Objects," *Art Theory*, 1965, last modified January 17, 2023, theoria.art-zoo.com/specific-objects-donald-judd/.

THE GREAT EXCAVATION:
BEGINNING WITH CLEAN OBSERVATION

102   **"you could do it with friends"**: William Finnegan, *Barbarian Days: A Surfing Life* (New York: Penguin Books, 2015), 18.

102   **"Style was everything in surfing"**: Finnegan, *Barbarian Days*, 334.

AN INNOVATION IN SEEING: USING THE LENS OF DOUBT

109   **"There are more animals living"**: Douglas Anderson, "Lens on Leeuwenhoek," 2014, last modified January 17, 2023, lensonleeuwenhoek.net/content/about-web.

110   **an autodidact with an affinity:** Richard Holmes, *The Age of Wonder: How the Romantic Generation Discovered the Beauty and Terror of Science* (New York: Vintage Books, 2008), 163–211.

113   **steeped in this same ideology:** Charles King, *Gods of the Upper Air: How a Circle of Renegade Anthropologists Reinvented Race, Sex, and Gender in the Twentieth Century* (New York: Anchor Books, 2020).

114   **phenomenon of "sound blindness"**: Franz Boas, "On Alternating Sounds," *American Anthropologist* 2, no. 1 (January 1889): 47–54.

114   **"will not become fruitful until"**: Franz Boas, "The Limitations of the Comparative Method of Anthropology," *Science* 4, no. 102 (1896): 901–8.

115   **chronically underfunded anthropology:** King, *Gods of the Upper Air*, 118–19.

116   **"The abductive suggestion"**: Charles Sanders Peirce, *Philosophical Writings of Peirce*, ed. Justus Buchler (Mineola, NY: Dover Publications, 2011), 304.

117   **"Do not block the way of inquiry"**: Peirce, *Philosophical Writings of Peirce*, 54.

120   **selling over 2,300,000 copies:** Pauline Kent, "Japanese Perceptions of *The Chrysanthemum and the Sword*," *Dialectical Anthropology* 24, no. 2 (June 1999): 181–92.

120   **"rather than a liability"**: Ruth Benedict, *The Chrysanthemum and the Sword: Patterns of Japanese Culture* (New York: Mariner Book, Houghton Mifflin, 2005), 10.

HOW TO LISTEN: PAYING ATTENTION TO SOCIAL SILENCE

123   **visiting his home in the foothills:** Pierre Bourdieu, *The Bachelors' Ball: The Crisis of Peasant Society in Béarn*, trans. Richard Nice (Chicago: University of Chicago Press, 2008).

124   **half of these young boys "unmarriageable"**: Bourdieu, *Bachelors' Ball*, 4.

126   **For generations, a peasant's social:** Bourdieu, *Bachelors' Ball*, 12–37.

127   **"market in symbolic goods"**: Bourdieu, *Bachelors' Ball*, 4.

127 **facing a "brutal devaluation":** Bourdieu, *Bachelors' Ball*, 4.

127 **"into a kind of total description":** Pierre Bourdieu, *Sketch for a Self-Analysis*, trans. Richard Nice (Chicago: University of Chicago Press, 2004), 61.

130 **I wanted to ask her about:** Gillian Tett, in conversation with the author. Gillian and I spoke on numerous occasions in 2021 and 2022, and I always took notes because she has so many interesting things to say. I also often turn to both of her books in my own observational processes for her insights: *The Silo Effect: The Peril of Expertise and the Promise of Breaking Down Barriers* (New York: Simon and Schuster, 2016) and *Anthro-Vision: A New Way to See in Business and Life* (New York: Avid Reader Press, 2021).

134 **"the worst financial crisis in global history":** Pedro Nicolaci da Costa, "Bernanke: 2008 Meltdown Was Worse Than Great Depression," *The Wall Street Journal*, August 26, 2014, wsj.com/articles/BL-REB-27453.

LOOKING FOR CULTURAL SHIFTS: HOW CHANGE HAPPENS

142 **"chains of equivalence":** Ernesto Laclau and Chantal Mouffe, *Hegemony and Socialist Strategy: Towards a Radical Democratic Politics*, 2nd ed. (London: Verso, 2014).

143 **"drawing in water":** Laclau and Mouffe, *Hegemony and Socialist Strategy*, 91–133.

152 **selling more than 220,000 vehicles:** Charles Riley, "The Great Electric Car Race Is Just Beginning," CNN Business, August 2018, last modified on January 17, 2023, cnn.com/interactive/2019/08/business/electric-cars-audi-volkswagen-tesla/.

154 **released its first F-150 electric vehicle:** "America's Bestselling Vehicle Now Electric," Ford Media Center, April 26, 2022, last modified on January 17, 2023, media.ford.com/content/fordmedia/fna/us/en/news/2022/04/26/production -begins-f-150-lightning.html.

155 **In June 2022:** "June 2022 Sales," Ford Media Center, June 2022, last modified on January 17, 2023, media.ford.com/content/dam/fordmedia/North%20America /US/2022/07/05/salesjune2022ford.pdf.

OBSERVING DETAILS: FINDING PORTALS TO INSIGHT

159 **"Suddenly there was something":** Robert A. Caro, *Working* (New York: Vintage Books, 2019), 143.

159 **"I think I realized":** Caro, *Working*, 143.

160 **"harsher kind of loneliness":** Caro, *Working*, 145.

160 **"What I decided to do":** Caro, *Working*, 145.

161 **"You find out things":** Caro, *Working*, 146.

161 **"No matter in what direction":** Robert A. Caro, The *Path to Power*, vol. 1 of *The Years of Lyndon Johnson* (New York: Vintage, 1990), 55.

162 **"In trying to analyze":** Caro, *Working*, 147.

162 **"There was something crucial":** Caro, *Working*, 154.

163 **interviewed a woman named Estelle Harbin:** Caro, *Working*, 155.

163 **"Then something occurred to me":** Caro, *Working*, 156.

164 **"It was something I had never":** Caro, *Working*, 156.

164 **"Of course he was running":** Caro, *Working*, 158.

169 **The novel's opening line:** Georges Perec, *Things: A Story of the Sixties* and *A Man Asleep*, trans. David Bellos and Andrew Leak (Boston: Verba Mundi, 2010), 21.

170 **"Where is the rest of it":** Georges Perec, "The Infra-Ordinary," in *Species of Spaces and Other Pieces*, ed. and trans. John Sturrock (New York: Penguin Classics, 2008), 5–6. Accessed on ubu.com, last modified on January 17, 2023, ubu.com/papers/perec_infraordinary.html#:~:text=What%20we%20need%20to%20question,ceased%20forever%20to%20astonish%20us.

170 **"What we must question":** Perec, "The Infra-Ordinary," 5–6.

171 **described in Saint-Sulpice:** Georges Perec, *An Attempt at Exhausting a Place in Paris*, trans. Mark Lowenthal (Cambridge, MA: Wakefield Press, 2010), 3.

171 **"My intention in the pages":** Perec, *Attempt at Exhausting*, 3.

171 **"Outline of an inventory":** Perec, *Attempt at Exhausting*, 5.

172 **"The 63 goes to Porte de la Muerte":** Perec, *Attempt at Exhausting*, 7.

172 **"blue bag / green shoes":** Perec, *Attempt at Exhausting*, 7.

173 **"What has changed here since yesterday":** Perec, *Attempt at Exhausting*, 29.

174 **"Make a list of the content":** Perec, "The Infra-Ordinary," 5–6.

EVERYTHING YOU NEED TO KNOW BEGINS WITH BIRDS

195 **"Science can never be enough":** J. A. Baker, *The Peregrine* (New York: New York Review of Books Classics, 2005), 6.

195 **"John Baker is 40":** Hilary A. White, "The Secret Life behind the Writer of England's Greatest Cult Book," *Irish Times*, January 6, 2018, last modified on January 19, 2023, irishtimes.com/culture/books/the-secret-life-behind-the-writer-of-england-s-greatest-cult-book-1.3333957.

196 **suffered in comparison:** Hetty Saunders, *My House of Sky: The Life and Work of J. A. Baker* (Dorset, UK: Little Toller Books, 2018), 122.

196 **"The hardest thing of all":** Baker, *The Peregrine*, 19.

196 **"Books about birds":** Baker, *The Peregrine*, 19.

196 **"The living bird":** Baker, *The Peregrine*, 19.

197 **"For ten years I have been":** Baker, *The Peregrine*, 12.

198 **"In my diary of a single":** Baker, *The Peregrine*, 14.

199 **"I shall try to make plain":** Baker, *The Peregrine*, 14.

199 **"The hawk's foot reached out":** Baker, *The Peregrine*, 50.

200 **"619 Peregrine kills":** Baker, *The Peregrine*, 29.

200 **quantifies only to reveal context:** Baker, *The Peregrine*, 26–32.

201 **"When hawks have gone from sight":** Baker, *The Peregrine*, 73.

201 **"These tables suggest":** Baker, *The Peregrine*, 26–27.

201 **"Predators that kill what is commonest":** Baker, *The Peregrine*, 27.

202 **meditative state of preparation:** Baker, *The Peregrine*, 23–26.

203 **what the hawk sees:** Baker, *The Peregrine*, 35–36.

205 **adjusts his behavior accordingly:** Baker, *The Peregrine*, 13–14.

205 **"We live, in these days":** Baker, *The Peregrine*, 95.

INDEX

Figures and photos are indicated by an *italic number*.

INDEX

INDEX

INDEX